488 ~~12~~ RULES

FOR LIFE

THE THANKLESS ART OF BEING CORRECT

~~12~~ 488 RULES FOR LIFE

THE THANKLESS ART OF BEING CORRECT

KITTY FLANAGAN

with fellow rule-makers
Sophie Braham Penny Flanagan
Adam Rozenbachs

Illustrations by Tohby Riddle

Andrews McMeel
PUBLISHING®

Andrews McMeel Publishing
a division of Andrews McMeel Universal
1130 Walnut Street, Kansas City, Missouri 64106
www.andrewsmcmeel.com

20 21 22 23 24 BVG 10 9 8 7 6 5 4 3 2 1

ISBN: 978–1–5248–6217–6

Library of Congress Control Number: 2020942137

First published in 2019 by Allen & Unwin, Australia

Original design by Tohby Riddle.
Design of U.S. edition: Sierra S. Stanton
Editorial adaptation: Lucas Wetzel and Kevin Kotur
Production: Margaret Daniels and Cliff Koehler

Neither the author nor the publisher has any connection with either Jordan Peterson, the author of 12 Rules for Life, or the publisher of that book, and readers should assume no such connection.

For Marmee

Contents

A Word from the Author

For the benefit of my North American readers, I'd like to explain two things. Firstly, I am an Australian comedian. Hopefully that will account for any odd references or language that might have slipped through the net. Secondly, this book was never supposed to be a real book. It was just a joke. An idea I came up with for a comedy segment on a TV show out here in Australia.

Inspired by Jordan Peterson's best-selling book, 12 Rules for Life, I went on air and declared that Mr. Peterson should have tried harder. Who has only twelve rules? For life? Man, I've got twelve rules just for the bathroom. I then presented my own book called 488 Rules for Life. We even mocked up the book and made a promotional video, which you can view online if you enjoy origin stories.

After the segment went to air, people started going into bookshops trying to buy this non-existent book. Turns out it's not just me who loves rules. Eventually one business-savvy bookseller contacted me to suggest I actually write the damn book so they could sell it. So I did. And here it is. But make no mistake, this book is still a joke. Even I admit that 488 is a lot of rules and I'm aware that no one is going to like all of the rules, but I'm pretty sure everyone will like some of the rules. And when you do hit a rule that resonates, you'll be surprised at how good it makes you feel. It's strangely comforting to know that you're not alone in being annoyed and irritated by those silly little things.

I think, deep down, people are crying out for rules. Once it was commonplace to look to published guides for advice on behavior, protocol, and etiquette. Guides produced by recognized authorities, such as Debretts in the United Kingdom and Emily Post in the United States.

But these days there is no such "Miss Manners" type guide in circulation. Perhaps that accounts for the rise in rude behavior and the increasing lack of basic courtesy in the modern world. If people don't know what the rules are, how are they supposed to abide by them?

Which is why I say, "Thank god for me." Now, with this comprehensive reference book at your fingertips, there can be no excuse for bad behavior. Whenever you're unsure about the right way to behave, whenever you want to know what not to do in any situation, simply turn to 488 Rules for Life. The answer is bound to be in here somewhere.

How to Use This Book

This book is divided into sections, and within each section you will find a range of rules. Some are fairly basic, things that everyone should already know; others are more specific and are for the people I call genuine rule enthusiasts. And occasionally you will come across rules so particular and persnickety that only absolute zealots like myself will be able to get on board. I have separated these into special sealed sections so that the more tolerant reader can avoid them easily.

Whatever level of rule disciple you are, know that reading this book and observing these rules will definitely make the world a nicer place. I also guarantee you will be better looking and better informed; in fact, you'll be a better human overall. So think of it as a self-help book, only you don't have to give up sugar, buy expensive exercise equipment, or keep a diary of your dreams. All you have to do is speak up when you see someone breaking the rules. A gentle but friendly reminder is all it takes:

"Hey buddy! Rule number 266—no sunglasses on the back of your neck, thanks man, just letting you know." There's no need to be rude or confrontational about it—keep it light. Remember, like me, you're here to help.

THE FUNDAMENTAL RULE

1
If you don't agree with a rule, forget about it; move on to the next one

Whatever you do, don't get angry and start bleating on social media about how it would be impossible to live your life by these 488 rules. That's not what this book is about.

AROUND THE HOME

GENERAL HOUSE RULES

2
Football jerseys are not art

Don't frame them. And definitely don't hang them on the wall.

3
Don't waste your money on surround sound

Nobody cares, guys. And I say guys because it is usually guys who insist on surround sound. When I'm watching TV, I find it weird if the sound isn't coming from the television. After all, the person walking on the television is *on the television*, in front of me, so it's really creepy to hear footsteps behind me or, indeed, all around me.

Same goes for those elaborate sound systems that people (again, usually men) install. The ones where they wire up the entire house with speakers in every room so they can pipe their tunage throughout. It's not a department store, it's just your house; you don't need the music to follow you around wherever you go. Spend your money on nice deli meat instead.

4
You don't need a media room or home theater

Just watch television in the living room like a normal person. Or go to the movies.

5
Supersizing is for beverages, not family portraits

There are many businesses that will blow up your family photo onto an enormous canvas, but that doesn't mean you should get one. A few regular-sized photos will do just fine; you don't want to turn your living room into some kind of in-memoriam shrine.

6
Don't complain about your housekeeper

Having a housekeeper is one of life's greatest luxuries, and if you can afford one you should be extremely grateful. And no matter how lax you might think your cleaner is, remember, it's still better than mopping your own kitchen floor or scrubbing your own bathroom and pulling your own disgusting hair-monster out of the drain.

7
Wait a week before accusing your housekeeper of stealing

People always accuse the housekeeper. Never to their face, but behind their back in hushed tones to their friends: "I think the housekeeper might have taken my necklace/favorite plate/ earring/five bucks/tape measure/spatula, etc."

Your housekeeper is not stupid; housekeepers know they will always be number one on the suspect list, which is why I guarantee the housekeeper did not take your stuff.

Here's the more likely scenario: you've put your necklace/ favorite plate/earring/five bucks/tape measure/spatula somewhere you don't usually put it and then you've done what all middle-aged people do—completely forgotten where you put it.

Give it a week; whatever the cleaner has "stolen" will turn up.

8
The toilet is not a magical trash can with water in it

A lot of people believe you can flush anything down the toilet, and technically you can flush a lot of things, be it a goldfish, a LEGO man, or a kilo of hash. But just because you can doesn't mean you should. Now, I don't have a college degree in toilets, so I consulted a toilet care professional (or plumber, as they are more commonly known) who told me in no uncertain terms that only three things should be flushed down the toilet: Pee. Poo. And paper. Not your leftover stew, not your failed sourdough starter, and definitely not your dead hamster. Give that little guy some dignity and a proper burial. Either that, or stick him in the regular trash.

9
Glamor shots belong in a drawer

First, think very carefully about whether you really need a soft-focus, glassy-eyed shot of yourself dressed in high heels and a feather boa, kneeling on a whorish-looking bed surrounded by red satin cushions. And then think even more carefully about whether you need to put that photo on display anywhere.

THE BATHROOM

10
Your bathroom must have a door

This sounds absurdly obvious, but there is a disturbing trend among fancy-pants architects at the moment to create en suite bathrooms with glass doors, or worse, *no* doors. I understand the desire to merge your indoor and outdoor spaces or to combine your living and dining room, but this open-plan bedroom-bathroom thing is nothing more than a seamless merger of pretension and gross impracticality (emphasis on the gross).

11
One sink is ample

No matter how much you and your partner love doing stuff together, there is absolutely no need to brush your teeth standing side by side, each with your own individual sink. Personally, I prefer to be alone in the bathroom no matter what I'm doing. However, if you happen to be one of those weird couples who like being in the bathroom together, abluting at the same time, then surely you are comfortable enough to spit into the same sink. Which means "twin vanities" are completely unnecessary. One bathroom, one sink.

12
Don't marinate in your own filth

The bathroom is not a library. There are far more pleasant, not to mention less smelly, places to read your book. Don't linger in there—get in, get out.

13
Replace the toilet paper roll

Just do it. You're a grown-up. It takes ten seconds.

14
Do not leave one square of toilet paper on the roll

Don't kid yourself, this is worse than not replacing the roll because of the effort required to leave that one square behind. Everyone knows it wasn't an accident, it was a carefully orchestrated event carried out in order to avoid replacing the roll. You pulled gently on the paper, taking great care not to unravel all of it and leave an empty roll. You may even have reverse-rolled it to make sure you left that one square on there: one square that you know perfectly well is of no use to anyone.

And don't be the dick that just sits the new roll on top of the empty roll, that doesn't count either.

15
Shut the bathroom door

I'll brook no argument or discussion about this one. If you are on the toilet, shut the bathroom door; it's a basic courtesy to other members of your household. No one should have to see anyone else mid-evacuation with their pants around their ankles. Parents with small children, you are the exception. I realize that toddlers like to be able to access you at all times and will often hammer relentlessly on a closed bathroom door, concerned and sometimes even alarmed about your sudden disappearance from view. (My dog is a bit the same.)

16
No talking on the toilet

The only words you should ever have to utter while on the toilet are "I'm in here" or "just a minute" in response to an enquiring knock on the door. Nothing is so important that it can't wait until you exit the bathroom. This rule is of particular concern in public restrooms. A lot of women love a gabfest in the can, somehow forgetting that there are germs flying around all over the place, and by flapping your gums and having a good old chitty chat, you are inviting those germs right into your mouth. Bottom line, if your butt is open, your mouth should be closed.

17
Don't take food or beverages into the can

Who'd have thought that ever needed to be said? But apparently it does. You know who you are (American guy called Tom who lives in Manchester and whom I witnessed take a newspaper and "hot cup of joe" into the bathroom).

18
The bathroom trash can is for bathroom trash only

Sometimes the bathroom waste basket is the closest. Perhaps you arrive home just as you finish eating a banana or a bag of Cheetos. On the way in, you pass by the bathroom and spy the trash can. You must forgo the urge to toss your empty wrappers into that trash can, no matter how convenient it is. Because what happens next is, when someone else uses the bathroom, they look down into the trash, see the banana skin and think, *Oh dear god, was Jeff eating a banana on the can? How disgusting!*

19
FPC—Flush. Pause. Check

Always wait after flushing so you can do a final check to make sure you are leaving nothing behind. Nothing. Not a mark, not a smear—there should be zero evidence of what's gone on in that bathroom. Don't leave a crime scene.

20
No phone calls on the toilet

The only thing worse than having a phone call with someone who is on the toilet is the realization that they are indeed on the toilet. It's usually something that dawns on you slowly. Probably because—for most normal people—the idea of making calls from the crapper is beyond comprehension, so it always takes a while to put all the pieces together. First you notice the strange echo-chamber effect, then come the oddly timed pauses and strangled grunts in their speech. "So I wondered if you ... *hnnnn* ... could let Margaret ... *hnnnnnnn* ... know that I might be late ... *hnn* ... today." And finally confirmation comes when you actually hear the waterfall cascading into the bowl or, worse, the splashdown. Unbelievable as it may seem, a lot of people take calls while on the toilet; I know because I hear them do it in public restrooms all the time. A phone rings and then the person actually answers it? "Yeah ... *hnnny*hello?" What is wrong with these people? The toilet cubicle is not a phone booth.

THE KITCHEN

21
The sink is not a dishwasher

These days most people have a dishwasher or, as I like to call it, a magic electric washy-washy box. And it really is magical, you can put anything in there and it comes out clean, requiring minimal effort on your part. Yet there are still people who think that dumping dishes in the sink, near the dishwasher, is good enough. It isn't. Either go the extra step (literally—the dishwasher is never more than a step away from the sink) and pop that sucker in the dishwasher *or* wash it up. They're your two options. Do not, however, just plonk it in the sink and think *"Well done me!"*

22
Everything can go in the dishwasher

Everything. No matter how big. Even if it takes ten minutes to rearrange everything in order to cram that saucepan or wok or blender jug in there, it's better than having to spend two minutes washing something up.

23
Flog the dishwasher until it does the job properly

Sometimes the dishwasher does a half-assed job and you find something that still has a bit of food stuck to it. When that happens, it's up to the dishwasher to make things right. Don't be a martyr and clean the dish or frying pan or wooden spoon yourself—that's rewarding the dishwasher for shoddy workmanship. Instead, you put whatever it is right back in the dishwasher and leave it there until it comes out clean. Whether it takes another two or another twenty wash cycles, it doesn't matter: the dishwasher has got to learn.

24
One person cooks, the other cleans up

In a couple or a family, the person who cooks the meal should never have to clean up as well. If you live alone, obviously this is not feasible; therefore, I suggest you try to cook as neatly as you can. However, I must stress that this "cook neatly" thing is a guideline, or recommendation, not a rule. As someone who lives alone and cooks like the Swedish chef from *The Muppets*, I cannot in all good conscience instruct anyone to "clean as you go."

25
Clean up the kitchen before you go to bed

Again, not really a rule, more of a note-to-self.

HEALTH & LIFESTYLE

A Word about Wellness

Wellness advocates and experts all claim they can improve your quality of life, whether it's by not eating sugar or by drawing toxins out of your body with hot cups and candles or by rubbing your face with dung because that's what some tribe did 5,000 years ago in a tiny part of Outer Mongolia. But sometimes I think we can get distracted by all the hype and forget to look at the bigger picture.

I was backstage at a corporate event once and witnessed a well-known anti-sugar crusader nibbling the dark chocolate coating off a single almond. She was scraping it off in tiny bits with her front teeth. It took her about twenty minutes. She noticed me staring (it was hard to look away, she was gnawing at that thing like a rat on a cable) and confessed that she allowed herself a minuscule amount of dark chocolate every day as her little reward. I told her quite smugly that I didn't allow myself any dark chocolate whatsoever. I didn't say; that's because dark chocolate is a punishment disguised as confectionery, rather I just enjoyed pretending I took my health more seriously than she did.

I know she looks better than me and I know she'll live longer than me, but my point about looking at the bigger picture is that I'm not sure I want to live longer if the only "treat" I'm allowed is one dark chocolate nut per day. Especially if I have to eat it hunched over in a corner like an obsessive-compulsive squirrel.

And for the record, I don't want to drink bone broth for breakfast or rub my face with dung either. I guess I just don't care enough about my own wellness—which is not a word, by the way—and you can read more about that in Language Rules.

INSPIRATION AND ADVICE

26
Cushions are not spiritual advisors

The current trend for putting trite advice on soft furnishings has to stop. No one has ever read *Live, Love, Laugh* on a pillow or *Dream, Relax, Feel* on a wall hanging and thought, *Oh what an excellent idea, I've not lived, loved, or laughed in ages. Well, that all changes right now, thank you, cushion!*

In fact, more often than not, I find these clichéd bon mots have the opposite effect and actually inspire rage and the desire to punch something, usually a cushion with the hateful *Keep Calm and Carry On* printed on it.

27
Never tell someone to "just imagine the audience naked"

This is one of the dumbest things you can ever say to a person who is about to do a bit of public speaking. There would be nothing more distracting than looking around a room and imagining what everyone looks like in the nude. How are you supposed to remember your speech when you're envisaging a room full of lumpy naked people?

28
Don't offer up clichés as advice

No one who has just been dumped wants to hear, "There are plenty more fish in the sea." It means nothing. If you must trot out this hoary old chestnut, then at least try to make it more accurate. "There are plenty more fish in the sea . . . *but* there are also a lot of bottom feeders and unpleasant smelly creatures that won't be to your taste at all, plus a few nasty aggressive types with big sharp teeth, so maybe the ocean's not the best place to go looking for a new partner."

29
"It is what it is" actually means "please stop talking"

When someone says, "It is what it is," they are not being wise and philosophical; rather, they are sick of listening to you and are trying to wrap up the conversation.

30
Life is not a sport so you don't need a coach

When life coaches first hit the scene, which I think was back in the nineties, it seemed like they were some kind of southern-Californian joke that would go away faster than the trend for walking with ski poles or using a PalmPilot organizer.

Life coaches, however, have not gone away—they have proliferated. And what has become apparent over the years is that, oftentimes, life coaches are people who have failed at other professions. So really the only advice a life coach should be doling out is: "If you want to turn your life around and become successful, you should become a life coach. Because then you can get paid to tell someone else how to turn their life around and become successful . . . by becoming a life coach."

Come to think of it, maybe that's exactly what they are doing and maybe that's why there are so many life coaches out there.

SMOKING

31
If you smoke, you smell

All the time. And that's OK, as long as you are aware of it. Sucking a mint only makes you smell like a smoker who has just sucked a mint. And washing your hands makes you smell like a smoker who has just washed their hands. Again, that's fine, just don't think you're fooling anyone.

32
If you vape, you look a lot less cool than you think

In fact, you look like you are blowing a USB stick. Or R2-D2's detachable penis.

EXERCISE GEAR

33
Only buy black leggings

Any other color simply makes a feature of the sweat around your box and crack. Pop on a pair of light gray leggings next time you exercise and you'll see that even when you barely break a sweat up top, downstairs you'll be showcasing a serious Rorschach inkblot test in your pants. That's why people in the gym are staring—they're either trying to work out what the stain resembles or, worse, they're wondering if you've wet yourself. Because it's difficult to tell the difference between sweat and pee, so there's a good chance you'll just look like a lady who went a bit too wide on her warrior pose and blew a piss-valve.

34
Stop calling it "active wear"

Most people I see wearing "active wear" are at the mall. So perhaps we should use the term "Lycra shopping outfit" instead.

35
Once you are no longer active, get changed

You may wear your exercise gear en route to the gym or the park or the hot yoga dojo or wherever you are going to be active. You may also keep it on as you make your way home again, and you may even detour to the store, briefly, to pick up a couple of things. But that's it. Once you're home, admit that you're not going to be doing any more lunges or downward dogs and that it's time to put on some less-active wear.

36
Dress according to the standard of cyclist you are

Many of us enjoy a spot of tennis, yet I never see anyone down at my local club sporting a full Serena Williams-style catsuit. Cyclists should bear that in mind and rethink their cycling gear. If you're not racing in the Tour de France, there's absolutely no need for those gut-hugging tops with multiple pockets all around that allow you to strap energy bars to yourself like dynamite on a suicide bomber vest.

You can probably live without those three bananas and four Clif Bars, not to mention the numerous electrolyte sachets. After all, you're only going to be riding for about an hour at the most. The larger part of your morning will be spent sprawled across multiple tables at the local cafe drinking lattes with all the other middle-aged men in padded ball-bag pants and zip tops covered in logos of sponsors who aren't actually your sponsors. And the reason they aren't your sponsors is because you're not a professional cycling team. You're just some dads in clip-cloppy shoes trying to get out of parenting on a Sunday morning.

37
Men must wear shorts over leggings

The gym is no place for people to discover whether or not you are circumcised. That's a private discussion for another place and time.

WORKING OUT

38
Lift less, more quietly

The odd noise of exertion here and there is fine, but if you are grunting and puffing and blowing your cheeks out to the point where bits of spit are starting to fly around, take some weight off, it's obviously too much for you.

39
Don't tell people you box

You participate in a boxing class. It's different.

40
No naked parading in the locker rooms

I don't care how good your body is, I don't want to see it striding from one end of the locker room to the other, or bending over while you rummage around in your gym bag for your matching bra and lacy thong set. You have a towel, use it.

41
No vigorous toweling

Pat or blot yourself dry after a shower. Don't rub yourself so hard that all your bits start wobbling and jiggling about. Just accept that it may not be possible to get yourself bone dry when you're in a communal locker area—that's why talcum powder was invented. Channel your inner old lady and throw a bit of lavendar talc around down there instead.

42
Keep two feet firmly planted on the ground at all times

Under no circumstances should you treat the locker room like a wood-chopping event. Don't even think about putting one foot up on the bench and then using that towel like a two-handed saw, going back and forth between your legs. If that's how you must dry yourself, wait for an individual stall to become available and have a go at yourself in private.

43
The park is not a gym

Take your kettle bells, your giant ropes, and your lumpy male trainers shouting, "Keep pushing Kimberleeeee, keep pushing!" and get out of what should be a lovely green space in which to relax, perambulate, picnic, or just play on the swings. (If you're a child, that is—please don't be one of those cutesy girl-women who giggles and gets her date to push her on the swing in a bid to be adorable.)

Bonus Rule
Yoga pants should not provide a "window" to your soul

When your leggings get a little threadbare and worn in the seat area, do the world a favor and throw them out. If in doubt, hold them up to the light. If you can see through them, so can everyone else when they're walking behind you. I don't mind how much junk you have in your trunk so long as I don't feel like I'm looking at it with x-ray specs. Sheer fabrics are for bridal veils, not ass cracks. Remember, when it comes to yoga pants, you want a solid thread count.

AGING GRACEFULLY

44
Old men should not have long hair

Cut the ponytail off, fellas. The bad news is, it probably wasn't even cool way back when you were young, but now it's even less cool *and* it's making everyone around you a bit sad.

45
Don't lie about your age

The number one thing to remember about getting older (aside from the fact that old men shouldn't have long hair) is that lying about your age is pointless. If you try to appear younger by knocking a few years off when you state your age, all anyone thinks is, *Wow, she looks dreadful!* or *Does this old bat think I'm stupid?*

When someone asks me how old I am, I prefer to add a few years rather than take them off. That way people will think, *Gee, she looks pretty damn good for sixty-five!* However, this trick doesn't always go according to plan. The inherent and ever-present danger is that when you tell someone you're sixty-five and you're really only forty-five, they may simply take you at your word and think, *Yeah, that seems about right.*

46
Put your feet away

Nothing gives away your age faster than cracked white heels and gnarly, split, yellow toenails. There is an odd phenomenon that occurs when men retire—for some reason they refuse to wear shoes anymore and instead decide to live out the rest of their lives in sandals. It's like suddenly they want everyone to bear witness to the hideous crime scene they have going on at the end of each ankle.

When I hit retirement age, I plan to petition the government for a senior citizen pedicure subsidy. A weekly pedicure for the elderly is a great idea. For a start, it prevents an old person's feet from turning into a pair of festering petri-dish experiments, but more importantly, it provides a much-needed social outing for lonely seniors. After all, the manicurist is the perfect captive audience, trapped at the business end of the pedicure chair while the old person chatters away.

47
Don't start singing like a Bee Gee

If you are having trouble hitting all the notes in your regular singing voice due to age, taking it up a notch and trying to sing in the key of "old lady falsetto" isn't going to help. Just turn your volume down and drone along quietly instead.

48
No one wants to hear about your ailments

That doesn't mean you have to stop talking about them, just be aware that there is not a person in the world who is interested, not even friends the same age as you. The only reason they willingly listen to you talk about your various afflictions is so they can carry on about their *own* ailments the minute your mouth stops moving. It's a bore exchange.

49
Leave the servers alone

Flirting with waiters half your age is unseemly and could also be viewed as a mild form of solicitation—because waiters will always be polite and oftentimes flirt right back—but it's only because they want a tip. Ergo, you're only getting their attention because you're paying for it.

Men, no matter what age they are, flirt with servers. They do it when they're young and they keep doing it when they get old. And they always think they're being incredibly charming. They're not. For women, however, flirting with servers is only something they tend to take up with enthusiasm once they hit middle age. It's like they've finally found their confidence and suddenly they think it's a bit cheeky and hilarious to hit on fit, young waiters. But it isn't. For, while the woman may see herself as a real cougar, all the waiter sees is a mangy old housecat yowling for attention.

50
Don't pretend you don't need glasses

If you're holding the menu at arm's length, you need glasses. If the font on your phone is billboard-sized and can be read by someone at the other end of the train car, you *really* need glasses.

51
Never make eye contact while eating a banana

After about the age of twelve, you need to be mindful of your banana consumption. What was once a fun fruit for monkeys and children suddenly becomes an undignified, innuendo-laden snack. Eat them in public if you must, but keep your eyes cast downwards.

52
Have a mirror right next to the front door

You might not want to look at your aging self, but remember, a mirror is your best friend. And having a mirror right next to the front door, preferably a magnifying mirror, should be mandatory for all people aged forty-five and over. Basically, you want to do a quick check before you leave the house. You're looking for renegade hairs, and they could be anywhere: upper lip and chin for ladies; ears and nose (inside and out) if you're a man. You want to remove anything that would transfix a small child and have them reaching out to tug it.

You also need to keep an eye out for those random straggly eyebrows that are so long you can only assume they've been growing out of your face since birth. How else do you explain the absurd length of them?

Once you're happy you're not leaving the house looking like the missing link, then do a quick once-over of your clothes, checking for any food spills. At a certain age, having a food stain down your front is the equivalent of having a sign around your neck that reads, *They're going to put me in a home soon.*

53
Men, don't dye your hair

For some reason, it just doesn't work for you. And most of you look pretty good gray anyway. Which, personally, I find quite annoying. Men with gray hair are always described as silver foxes—people use words like "sophisticated" or "Clooney-esque." Whereas when I allow my hair to go gray, the only celebrity I resemble is Meryl Streep in *Into the Woods*.

AT THE OFFICE

A Word about Open Offices

It has been a long time since I've had a "real" job and worked full time in a "real" office. My most recent in-office experience was at the ABC—the Australian Broadcasting Corporation—while working on the show that spawned this book. No matter what department you work in at the ABC, you are forced to endure an open office. There is one exception, of course: Up on the executive floor. There you will find a magical place with plenty of walls and doors which, I imagine, must really annoy the managers and bosses forced to work in such private conditions. After all, they're the ones who constantly champion the open plan system and tell the rest of us how great it is.

When I arrived at the ABC and discovered the office was an open office, I decided to work from home. This was not an arrangement I came to with management; rather, it was the only way I could get any work done. I never told anyone I was working from home; instead, I came in every morning, put my jacket on the back of my chair, scattered a few notes across

my desk, placed my bag underneath, then took what I needed
and went home to do some work. I was able to get away with
this because at the time I lived only ten minutes down the road.
So if I got a text or a call saying, "Where are you?" or "Can
you come to the meeting room for a read-through?" I would
reply, "Sure, just grabbing a coffee, back in ten. Smiley face
emoji, coffee cup emoji, heart emoji, two exclamation marks."

Ultimately, I was far more productive working from home
than I would have been sitting out in the open among thirty
other employees, a lot of whom were making necessary but still
very distracting phone calls and some of whom were making
distracting and completely unnecessary phone calls.

It did mean there was a fair bit of driving back and forth—
which gives rise to my argument that the open-plan office model
is not only highly unproductive thanks to the miserable employees
it creates, but in my case it also contributed to global warming
because of the time I spent on the road burning fossil fuels.

GENERAL OFFICE RULES

54
Don't take your wang out at the office, ever

I realize this seems incredibly obvious, but in the current climate, with everything that's come to light about men sending dick pics, wanking in front of female colleagues or into potted plants, and showing off their knobs to coworkers like you would a new iPhone etc., apparently we do need to spell this one out. So here it is again:

55
Your penis should remain in your pants during office hours

Unless you are ALONE in a toilet stall using it to pee—then it can come out—but please, put it away as soon as you're done.

56
During office hours, turn your phone to silent

It's common courtesy; no one in the office wants to hear your Stevie Wonder, "I Just Called To Say" ringtone, in full, every time your phone rings. No one. Not even Stevie W.

57
Go easy on the reply-all button

We all get enough rubbish filling up our inboxes, we certainly don't need to be included in irrelevant reply-all chains. Just because someone emailed a question to the entire office doesn't mean you have to reply-all; just reply to the person who sent the email.

58
Don't insert yay into Friday

No matter how happy you are that the week has ended, there's no need to resort to using office clichés like "Friyay." Especially in pointless inter-office group emails: *Happy FriYAY everyone!* Everyone knows it's Friday. Everyone knows the weekend is coming. Everyone is happy. No one's mood is buoyed by your arbitrary yaying.

"Hump Day" is similar to Friyay, in that there's never any call for it. If you can't think of anything to say to an associate in your office besides "Happy Hump Day!" just give them a polite nod and pass without saying anything. It's not compulsory to speak every time you pass one another. See rule 63 for clarification on the correct way to greet coworkers.

59
Stop the senseless "e-meeting"

Don't write "pleased to e-meet you" at the top of an email. You lost me at "e"—I'm not reading any further.

60
Team bonding activities should be optional

Some people love it when management decides that an afternoon of bowling or paintballing or (god forbid) karaoke will help everyone work better as a team. Others would rather be dead. So respect the rights of those who hate "forced fun," which also includes themed "dress-up days." Not everyone cares about the playoffs or even owns a football jersey. And maybe Tammy from accounting is self-conscious about her broad caboose and doesn't want to wear jeans on *any* day, let alone on

Jeans for Genes Day when she'll feel even more conspicuous in her sheets-of-denim being compared to everyone else in their teeny-tiny skinny jeans.

61
Don't attempt humor in signs around the office

The problem with the jokey sign is that it does not withstand repeat viewings. People go to the kitchen or bathroom several times a day and there's no way your note is funny enough that folks will enjoy it and chuckle every time they see it. What you should aim for in an office note is mild terseness. You do this by employing shouty caps and underlining:

PUT YOUR DISHES IN THE DISHWASHER—PLEASE

But avoid doing "gags" like taking a poster of a cute pussycat and writing the following underneath it:

WASH YOUR CUP OR THIS KITTEN GETS IT!

And if you need to put up signs in the bathroom, humor should be the last thing on your mind. When I visit an office and see a sign like this in the bathroom:

IF YOU SPRINKLE WHEN YOU TINKLE,
BE A SWEETIE, WIPE THE SEATIE

I'm not thinking, *Oh that's funny, 'cos it rhymes*, I'm thinking, *Who in god's name is pissing on the seat so often that a sign is required?* After all, I'm in the ladies restroom. To the best of my knowledge, ladies sit down to use the toilet and it is physically impossible to pee on the seat when you are sitting *on* that seat. If women are somehow spraying it around like tom cats in your office bathroom, the time for joking is long past; the only sign that should go up is one that says:

HEY LADIES, <u>SIT DOWN</u>

62
No personal calls in open-plan offices

In this unfortunate, modern world of open-plan offices, it surprises me that I have to articulate this as a rule. I assumed everyone was like me and got really self-conscious making personal phone calls when other people were within earshot. Turns out, some people aren't the slightest bit embarrassed about others overhearing their personal calls; in fact, they seem to revel in it. I witnessed one woman FaceTiming her young children from her open-plan office desk every day at around five o'clock. Perhaps it was her way of justifying staying late at the office. I say, if you miss your kids so much that you have to FaceTime them, just go home.

63
One proper greeting per day is ample; after that, a nod will suffice

Working in an office can be stressful. Not only do you have to get your work done, you must also make an effort to socialize with your fellow employees, especially when you find yourself trapped together in the claustrophobic staff kitchen. At times it can feel as though your whole day is taken up both asking and answering bland questions like "How was your weekend?" or "Got any plans this weekend?" or "Hungover much? Heh heh."

The point is that between regular trips to the kitchen, the bathroom, and even the printer (to pick up those personal documents you've been printing out at work) you will cross paths with your coworkers multiple times a day. This means multiple greetings per day, and it's not surprising that these become less enthusiastic as the day wears on. That's why it's okay to simply nod at your coworkers, or even just raise an eyebrow of acknowledgment from the second interaction onward. It's too exhausting to have to come up with new small talk for each passing, and if you're not careful you can end up falling into the "say what you see" trap (I am one of the worst offenders of this) passing someone in the corridor and saying something like "Ooh, having a cup of tea" or "Mm, a cookie. Good stuff."

Others try to cover their awkwardness by attempting humor, failing, then laughing at their "joke" anyway: "Heyyy, nice green top, Ellen ... did you see Sophie's wearing a green top today too? Sorry guys, I didn't get the memo! Ha ha ha."

Remember, if you have nothing of substance to say, it's perfectly okay to go full Ronan Keating and say nothing at all.

64
No hot-desking

Hot-desking is sometimes referred to as "an agile office." It's like an open office, but even more shitty. You are forced to cart all your belongings around with you like a Bedouin and "find" a free desk to work at each day. Then you must completely clear that desk of all your things at quitting time. Leave no file behind. I see it as a form of employee abuse. And in years to come, I hope there is a class action where all the people who have been forced to hot-desk take their employers to court and sue them for damages. I conducted an informal survey of the newsroom at the ABC that revealed that no one enjoyed it. No one. Not one person said, "Yes, I quite like not having anywhere permanent to put my things. It's also great not being able to personalize a space that I spend at least eight hours a day in. But most of all, I like never knowing where to find anyone. It adds an element of discovery to my work life."

Incidentally, the more common term for hot-desking is "shit-desking" and it's been proven in numerous studies, far more formal and official than mine (I just went around asking, "On a scale of one to ten how much do you hate hot-desking?") that it does not improve employee productivity. Quite the contrary, in fact. While you might save money buying less furniture and office space, you lose money by having unhappy, less-efficient employees. I call #Time'sUp on hot-desking.

65
Comedy dancing is not dancing—just don't dance

This is a rule for all the office jokers at the office Christmas party.

FOOD IN THE OFFICE

66
Don't eat at your desk

This is controversial, I know, but my reason is twofold. Firstly, everyone is entitled to a lunch break. This should be an hour (or half hour) where you break and go for lunch. It's not at all cryptic. A lunch hour should not mean an hour spent at your desk with lunch in one hand, still working with the other, dropping bits of food into your keyboard and using your pants as a napkin.

Secondly, it's incredibly unhygienic to eat at your desk and it's unpleasant for your fellow workers to witness, especially if you're eating something stinky like a hard-boiled egg or something noisy like a potato-chip sandwich. No judgment for eating a chip sandwich, by the way, that's an excellent carb on carb choice, just do it in a designated food-eating area.

67
No stinky foods in the office

Respect those around you and don't bring your leftover fish curry to work and then heat it up in the office microwave. No one wants to spend the afternoon working in the noxious fishy miasma you've just created. And while I understand that many people love tuna for its healthful and nourishing properties, I think we can all agree that it really does stink so, if you must eat it, I suggest going outside to enjoy your lunch in the open air. Don't chow down in the confines of the office where the windows only open a few inches, if at all. As for bringing french fries into the office, that is not just smelly, it's also mean. Because for the first thirty seconds, fries smell delicious and now you've made everyone in the office want fries. However, pretty soon those fries will turn cold and the office will smell like every teenage McDonald's employee when they come home from a shift reeking of cold grease and congealed fat.

68
No food in meetings

We're all busy. But if you're so busy that you're bringing soup to a meeting and slurping it during proceedings, then you need to organize your day better. Either reschedule the meeting or reschedule your soup slurping.

69
Pick one day a month to do birthday cake

Office birthday cake is a minefield. Yes, cake is great but not everyone is in the mood to drop everything and suddenly gather in the conference room at some random time of day whenever it's someone's birthday. There's never a set time for birthday cake, quite often it's a case of "Hurry up everyone, we're doing cake now because Jo is leaving early to go to a conference!" It's even less appealing when you know your only reward will be ten minutes of awkward forced togetherness and a piece of wet supermarket mud cake that you end up pushing around a paper plate with a plastic fork. I am, however, not against birthdays or cakes. My solution is to pick a day—one day a month, for argument's sake, let's say the last Friday of every month. Then on that Friday at 11:00 a.m. everyone gathers in the boardroom and someone reads out a list of all the people who have celebrated a birthday that month. Cake is presented, "Happy Birthday" is sung (in accordance with the following rule) and everyone enjoys a bit of cake with their morning coffee.

This allows cake to remain special, it also means everyone in the office knows when birthday cake day is approaching. You can schedule it into your workday, you can set your palate for cake, you can even stop work at 10:55 to make a cup of tea to go with your pending piece of cake. The other great advantage of this system is that it provides enough lead time for someone to actually make a decent cake. Surely that is preferable to the office intern being dispatched to Walmart to procure some hideous-looking cake encased in a plastic dome every time someone reveals it's their birthday.

70
Stop singing after the final "Happy Birthday to you"

No one wants to hear the "For he's a jolly good fellow" extended mix featuring MC Daryl the Office Good-Time Guy on "hip hip hoorays." It's awkward. People have work to do. And cake to eat. Hopefully a delicious homemade one if you've adhered to the previous rule.

LANGUAGE

GENERAL LANGUAGE RULES

71
Once you hear a word used in an ad, it's time to stop using it

A good example of this would be "hangry," which was used in a flavored-milk ad. You don't want to use that word anymore, because if it's appeared in an ad it's officially past its use-by date. Advertising people are notorious for being one step behind and stealing ideas from other art forms, such as films, TV, and comedy. I know because I used to be in advertising.

72
Never tell someone you have a GSOH

It's unnecessary. If you have a good sense of humor, it will become apparent the minute you say something funny or laugh appreciatively at something funny that someone else has said.

Similarly, you should never use the terms "dark" or "unique" to describe your own sense of humor. People who genuinely have a dark sense of humor don't think of it as dark, they just think of it as regular. Whereas people who *say* they have a dark or unique sense of humor are often trying to make themselves seem interesting, or justify the fact that no one laughed at something they said: "Oh, you don't get it? Must be because I have a very dark sense of humor."

73
Don't ever "wonder what the poor people are doing"

It's no big mystery. They're probably thinking about where their next meal is coming from or how they're going to pay their rent.

74
Stop saying "First World problems"

If you live in the First World, this phrase is an oxymoron. All of our problems are First World problems. So you can safely just say "problems." Unless, of course, you are suddenly hit with a Third World problem, then you might want to flag it as such: "Hey?! This bowl of sorghum is tasteless, and I think it's been made with polluted water, talk about Third World problems!"

Or if someone says to you: "I can't come in to work today, I've got cholera."

Then you can respond: "Wow! Third World problem or what?!"

75
Clown is not a verb

It's bad enough that you are a clown, please don't try to talk it up by saying that you are going to do some "clowning" or that you learned "to clown" in Paris.

76
You can't "verse" people

You can play against or "versus" someone. But "I'm versing you" sounds like you're aggressively reciting poetry at them.

77
Don't refer to your wife as "the boss"

As in "I'll have to check with the boss." Apart from anything else, it's almost always disingenuous and only ever cited by men who would overrule their "boss" in a heartbeat if she said something that didn't suit them.

78
Avoid using adjectives such as delicious or yummy in non-food contexts

For example, you can say, "This food is delicious." But you cannot say, "My, my, don't you look yummy today."

79
Don't describe inanimate objects as "sexy"

A typeface isn't sexy. Nor is an iPhone. Home renovation show judges are flagrant in their disregard for this rule, always referring to things like tap fittings or marble bench tops or even 2PAC polycarbonate cupboards as "sexy."

80
Keep more ye olde words in circulation

Don't try to keep up with the youth (see next section); instead, go back in time and choose words and phrases from the past. The English language is full of great gear and it's good to keep words alive. Words like "stepping out" and "courting" are so much better than "hooking up" or "getting with." I have always preferred "paramour" to boyfriend or girlfriend. And "poppycock" speaks for itself—what a great word. And while the Australian youth might refer to "caps, pingas, and nangs" (although they probably don't anymore but they did at the time I wrote that sentence), I think when it comes to drug language you can't go past words like "jazz-cabbage" or indeed the very old-fashioned and rather quaint "pot." The idea of going up to a dealer and asking for "three packets of pot, please" really tickles me.

81
Wellness is not a word

I know this word is everywhere now, it's inescapable, but it's as dumb as saying "healthosity" or "nutritionative."

82
The word "budget" should never be paired with any of the following

- Seafood
- Airline
- Plastic surgery
- Dental work

83
Don't refer to your "tribe"

Unless you are from an indigenous culture and you genuinely have a tribe. Note: a beard and strident opinions about cold-pressed coffee do not constitute a tribe.

84
Adults do not get to say "din-dins" or "nom-noms"

Remember, other people are trying to eat, don't ruin their appetite.

85
Don't ever mention your "happy place"

To me, this sounds less like a pleasant, fun state of mind and more like some kind of utopian wank palace you've had built in the basement.

86
Once you turn sixty, start every anecdote with "Stop me if I've told you this already"

It's the humanitarian thing to do. It means no one loses the will to live listening to your stories, and it ensures you remain a welcome guest rather than that repetitive bore everyone tries to avoid.

A Word about the Generation Gap

Youth-speak is an area of language that changes faster than any other, therefore it's difficult to make definitive rules about particular words you should or shouldn't use. That's because while youths are great inventers of words and phrases, they also dump those words as fast as they invent them. A basic rule of thumb for anyone over forty who wants to avoid looking out of touch is to listen closely to the vernacular of teenagers and then never use any of the words you just heard. Let the youth enjoy their own language; you have lots of other things, like financial stability and Facebook. (Which, of course, you totally stole from the youth because they were forced to drop it once all the parents and unhappy middle-aged married people discovered it and started using it to track down their high school sweethearts.) Act your age and maintain your dignity by sticking with language from your own era. As embarrassing as it may be to refer to something as "bitchin" or "bodacious," at least you just sound old, as opposed to old and try-hard.

Remember, if you have to ask a youth what the word means, you shouldn't use it. I have listed a few examples here, but this is by no means a definitive list. Also, they were listed at the time of writing, which means that by the time of publication, they may well have disappeared into the vast abyss of discarded youth-speak. The fact that I have heard some of them creeping into use on television suggests they are already out.

Lit. For the record, I don't know what it means. From the context in which I have heard it used, I gather it is something positive. But that's as much as I can tell you. And again, it's not my business to know. I'm well over forty.

* *Editor's note: The word "lit" was recently spotted in a well-known fried chicken chain billboard so it's safe to say "lit" is now obsolete.*

Dropped. Pertaining to music, such as a single or an album. If you grew up in a time when big black circles called records were released and shiny silver things called CDs came out, then you are too old to start telling me that someone's new album is "dropping." You should also never refer to "dropping a beat." Ever.

Banging. You can't erase your middle-agedness simply by listening to young people's radio stations. Sure, you can tune in as a way of staying across current musical trends, but avoid repeating any of the language you hear spoken by the presenters, such as "Wow, this shit is on fire" and "That song is banging!" Youth presenters, however, always drop their g's so it would actually be pronounced bangin', not that it matters because you won't be saying it.

Vibe Check. Any parent thinking of popping their head around their kid's bedroom door and saying, "Vibe check?" Don't. Stick with the classics. Like a simple "How's it going?" or "Leave the door open please," or "So this is where all the goddamn towels are! On the floor in your bedroom?!"

That said, the youth do not get a free pass on language just because they are young and inventive. There are still some rules and even some words I'd suggest they cut from their lexicon altogether, as you will see in the following section.

$$\longrightarrow$$

KIDS TODAY

87
Curb your use of the word "like"

Like is many things; however, it is not an adverb and should not be used as such:

And so I was, **like**, I cannot believe you are not going to, **like**, eat the dessert I made. And she was, **like**, but it's banoffee pie, which is, **like**, disgusting. It's, **like**, not even pie, it's banana-flavored mucus on, **like,** a cheesecake base. And I was, **like**, whatever.

As you can tell from the above, I don't particularly **like** banoffee pie.

88
Assume that people know what you mean

Unless you are explaining the solution to a quadratic equation, or you happen to speak in riddles worthy of a cryptic crossword, then it's safe to assume that most people will be able to follow what you're saying. So there's really no need to keep checking in and saying "Know what I mean?" every couple of sentences.

89
Don't use words you don't need, like "literally"

Most of us don't speak in metaphor and simile, we almost always speak literally, so there is rarely the need to qualify your sentence by adding the word "literally." As in "Oh my god, she ate the whole piece of cake, like, literally the whole piece of cake."

It would be highly unusual for someone to assume that "piece of cake" meant something else in this instance so you can do away with the word "literally."

However, if you were talking about your dog and how he chewed up one of your board games, then in that instance you might want to qualify your statement with a "literally": "We were playing Yahtzee the other day and then Bongo came along and ate the whole box and dice, literally the whole box and dice."

CONVERSATION

Conversation is the mainstay of any social event, be it a date, dinner party, or work function. It's something we get to practice all the time, yet very few of us are any good at it and I include myself here. I can talk for an hour and a half on stage at people no problem, but it's very different in social situations.

I get particularly nervous at parties. I have a real knack for grinding the conversation down into a series of dull questions that the other person has no interest in answering. I've noticed I also ask "closed questions" a lot of the time, questions that require a short one or two-word answer and never lead to a broader discussion. I know for a fact that I am often "that person," the one you get trapped talking to and have to invent an excuse to get away from. My saving grace is that I'm aware of my shortcomings, and when I sense I am dragging someone into one of my conversation death spirals, I will try to help them get away. I will be the one who suggests they move on, saying something like, "Look, I won't keep you, please go and get yourself a drink," while magnanimously gesturing at the bar with an extended arm, thereby showing them the exit route.

A truly good conversationalist has an uncanny knack of making the person they are talking to feel interesting. It's an amazing skill—usually you don't even realize you're in the presence of a good conversationalist, you just start thinking, Gee I'm telling some good stories today. Good conversationalists are few and far between, which is a shame because they make social occasions an absolute joy.

Obviously, as a person completely lacking in conversation skills, I needed to consult some experts to help formulate the following rules. Luckily I know a couple of excellent conversationalists.

One is my best friend Glenn. Another is my fellow rule-maker Sophie. I also know a third expert called Dan, a colleague whom I see only occasionally but who never fails to make me feel both interesting and interested. I have watched him have animated and lively discussions with anyone and everyone in a room, including people I would have written off as dull and boring. I reached out to him by email to ask for his tips on how to be a good conversationalist, but he didn't reply. I can only assume he was too engrossed in a conversation to answer me.

90
Turn-take

This is the basic rule of conversation. You each take a turn to speak. And you each take a turn to listen. This second bit is quite important. Listening is different from just watching the other person's mouth and waiting for it to stop moving so you can start talking again.

91
The onus is on you to make the conversation interesting

Don't immediately write someone off as boring; most people have something interesting to say and, if you can find a way to ask good questions, you should be able to have an interesting conversation with anyone.

92
Don't interrogate

The vibe you're going for in a conversation is "gentle inquisition." No one wants to feel like they're being cross-examined at a murder trial. Subtle coaxing to extract further detail is permissible, but don't badger them like a lawyer going after an uncooperative witness.

93
Keep your questions to ten words or less

You're not on NPR trying to expose a politician for misuse of public funds.

94
Move on rather than resort to air-filler phrases

Sometimes, despite the best of intentions, you just run out of stuff to say. Always move on before you start filling the awkward silence with phrases like "Ahhh, what a day" or *"C'est la vie"* or "Well, here we are."

95
Don't ask vegetarians why they are vegetarian

It's a question that they are forced to answer every time they sit down for a meal with a new person. It's boring for them and if you're lucky they will shut you down with a noncommittal shrug and a vague "I just prefer not to eat meat." But if you're unlucky you'll come up against a fundamentalist who will redirect the question right back at you and ask why you're NOT vegetarian. They will then rail at you about cruelty to animals, about how your love of meat is destroying the planet, and basically make you feel really guilty about your choices. Either way, there's no satisfactory answer so don't waste anyone's time, including your own, asking the question.

The exception is if you're talking to comedian Dave Hughes, who has quite an interesting answer, which relates to the fact that he used to work in an abattoir and it put him off eating meat for life. It will probably put you off eating meat too, not necessarily for life but at least for a couple of days, so that's good—you can do your bit for the planet, even if it's just for a day or two.

96
Always, however, ask converts why they converted

There is something quite bizarre about grown-up people with solid, tertiary educations converting to one of the traditional book religions. As someone who grew up Catholic and experienced the pointless rituals and praying firsthand, I have never understood how a rational, thinking adult can choose to adopt formalized religion. It's different when you're born into it; you don't know anything else and besides, it's your family, it's your culture.

97
Know when the small talk well is running dry and bail out

"Got any travel plans?" is an acceptable question when you're struggling to sustain a floundering conversation; however, if you then follow it up with "Oh that's nice . . . so, when do you leave?" the conversation is officially dead in the water. So make an excuse and exeunt. Unless you're planning a burglary of their house, there is nothing to be gained by garnering the exact dates of an acquaintance's holiday.

98
Recounting a TV series to someone in great detail does not constitute good conversation

I do this a lot. Sorry everyone.

99
Have a few emergency "go-to" questions
for when the conversation stalls

Basic conversation starters like:

"Who do you fancy to win the Australian Open?"

or

"What's your favorite soup recipe?"

or

"Would you rather be deaf or blind?"

or

"If you could ask Jennifer Aniston one question, what would it be?"

or

"Hand on heart, if you'd had an attic, would you have let Anne Frank hide in there?"

Bonus Rule
You must be in the same room to converse

You can't just shout at someone who is in another part of the house. They can't hear you. (Would somebody please tell my parents.)

PLANES, TRAINS & AUTOMOBILES

A Word about Air Travel

I admit I seem to have an excessive amount of rules pertaining to planes and airports, but that's because I do a lot of touring and I spend an excessive amount of time on planes and in airports.

I realize there are many people who only fly occasionally, and when they do it's almost always for the purpose of a vacation. That puts you in a completely different mindset to those who travel for work purposes. Being in vacation mode means you are far more likely to be in a good mood—you're going somewhere you've been dreaming about, you have no urgent or pressing engagements at the other end—and all that adds up to a person who is far more relaxed and far less likely to get apoplectic about cockheads who stand too close to the baggage carousel. In fact, you might even be one of those cockheads.

FLYING

100
No reclining on short flights

It's already a tight fit on a plane, even for me, and I'm well below average height. For this reason, we must all be a little selfless on planes and consider our fellow travelers, in particular the passenger in the seat directly behind us. If the flight is short, say two hours or less, then sit up. The whole way. Do not recline. After all, if you're *that* tired, you'll be able to fall asleep sitting up. No need to recline with a pillow and a blankie, it's not like you're going to be in the air long enough to enjoy a bit of solid REM sleep. So just sit up and do what all the other more considerate travelers do—doze off for a few minutes and then wake up with a jerk when their head nods forward.

101
Put your kid's seat up and keep it up

Under no circumstances should small children be allowed to recline their seat. This is totally unnecessary and quite possibly the single greatest cause of air-rage on passenger planes today.

102
No bare feet on planes

The only time your feet should be bare is when you are removing one sock in order to place a heavier (or lighter) travel sock on instead. You definitely should not be walking around the cabin in bare feet, and as for going to the restroom barefoot, that is an absolute no-no. Shoes should always be slipped back on for trips to the restroom because I don't know what people are doing in there, but I know they're doing it all over the floor.

103
Apparently the person in the middle seat gets both armrests

I confess I did not know this rule; it came courtesy of a well-informed flight attendant, so I guess it must be true. It makes sense—there is nothing more punishing than the middle seat, so you deserve some kind of reward and that is both armrests. Apparently.

104
Headphones, headphones, headphones

This is another of those rules that you wouldn't think needed to be stated. Surely, as considerate humans, we have a natural-born instinct to always wear headphones on a plane. Not the case, it turns out. I was on a plane recently where the young woman in front of me was watching a movie on her iPad with no headphones. After doing a lot of loud "tsking" and getting no response, I finally leaned forward and asked her, very passive-aggressively, if she would like some headphones, and even proffered a set of the complimentary plane headphones at her. She blithely waved me away and chirpily said, "No, thank you." And I sat back and felt sad. I can't blame her—it's the parents' fault. Headphone usage is something that needs to be taught from an early age. I would suggest that after a child has learned "Mama" and "Dada," their next words should be "headphones, please."

I am not one of those extremists who advocates for child-free flights; I think that's ridiculous. Rather, children should be welcomed on planes, but the airlines need to take more responsibility and include the headphone rule in the safety briefing.

Because it really is a safety issue. I am perfectly happy to play peek-a-boo with your toddler over the back of the chair; I don't even mind if your kid wails a bit. I get it, they're just kids, they get upset about stuff like spilled apple juice and broken crayons. But god help you if you let your kid watch *Peppa Pig* or play some game on an iPad without headphones. I will have you arrested by the sky marshal. And if there's no sky marshal on board then I'll tell the flight attendant I overheard you say you have a bomb in your bag.

105
Always nudge a snoring passenger awake

It's perfectly acceptable to "accidentally" bump a snoring passenger in order to wake them up. In fact, if you are seated next to the snorer, it's your duty to give them a sharp elbow nudge. Snoring passengers have no right of reply; they cannot object to getting nudged. This is another problem that would be better dealt with by the airlines themselves, to prevent any argument or awkwardness between passengers. My suggestion is that a flight attendant should occasionally patrol the aisles with a stick to poke any snoring passengers awake.

106
Do not, under any circumstances, have sex in the restroom

What is wrong with people? If anyone ever boasts to me about how they've joined the "Mile High Club," my only thought is, *Ewwwww, you had sex in a tiny cramped toilet that four hundred-odd people have been pooing and peeing in. You disgust me.*

*Author's Note: All these flying rules were originally written pre-COVID-19 and were hailed as compulsory reading for airline passengers. That was well before we'd heard of wet markets and pangolins. When this updated U.S. edition went to print, many airlines were still grounded. However, there will come a time when we are all back in the air, and when that happens, I suggest that the following two rules be passed into law. Or at least be included on the seat-back pocket safety card.

107
Maximum three sniffs, then get a tissue

This is a universal rule, but nowhere is it more important than on a plane, where those around you are trapped in their seats and unable to move away from your incessant and unrelenting sniffing.

108
Accept the lozenge

Even before the 2020 pandemic, whenever someone coughed on a plane, it would put me on edge. After all, it's a very limited amount of air we're all sharing up there. And my assumption was that those coughed-up germs would soon be blowing directly onto my face courtesy of that little outlet above my head. The longer the coughing went on, the more panicky I would become. By the time the pilot landed that flying bacteria tube, I'd be convinced everyone on board was infected with SARS or swine flu or even good old-fashioned Ebola. Ohhh remember those viruses? The ones we did manage to contain? Bleeding from the eyeballs with Ebola seems almost quaint now, doesn't it? Point is, if there was ever a cougher on board, I would make a mental note of the seat number they were in so that when the plane landed,

I could inform the authorities that patient zero was in seat 9A. I've watched enough biohazard movies to know it's imperative they be able to identify where the epidemic started.

My extreme paranoia about coughing on planes means I always carry lozenges. Not only because I don't want to be the cougher on the plane, but also so that I am in a position to offer the cougher a lozenge. It's the polite way of saying, "For the love of god, you're going to kill us all. Stop coughing!" So remember, if you are ever offered a lozenge, please take it.

109
Keep walking when you hit the moving walkway

Moving walkways are designed to make your journey through the airport a little faster, to speed you along as you walk. However, most people use them to see what life would be like if they lost the use of their legs. The minute they hit that moving rubber walkway, they stop dead, no longer able to put one leg in front of the other.

110
No bunching

Ordinarily, Australians (and, I would say, Americans too) are pretty good about respecting one's personal space. But for some reason all bets are off at airports. Something about the proximity to planes brings out people's inner urge to bunch right up behind you. It begins as soon as you line up to check in. Suddenly people start bunching up, "accidentally" nudging their luggage into the backs of your legs. And the bad news is the bunching doesn't stop until you actually leave the airport at the other end of your journey. If we are to get anything positive out of COVID-19, let it be that bunching at airports is finally declared against the law.

111
Only people in the aisle seats may stand up before the door is opened

When the plane lands and the seatbelt sign goes off, usually what happens is everyone leaps up and tries to move out into the aisle; however, you must only do that if you are seated *on* the aisle. Everyone else needs to wait patiently in their seats. You can stand up, if you're short like me and won't hit your head, but you can't move out into the aisle. You physically can't. It's Archimedes's displacement principle—you can't just keep pouring more bodies into the aisle without it overflowing. And there's nowhere for it to overflow to until they open the door at the front of the plane.

So stop thinking you can defy science and accept that there is only one way to get off a plane and that is single file, in an orderly fashion, row by row, once the door is actually opened. If you are seated in the last row of the plane, you're getting off last, there's nothing you can do about it, that's just how it works.

112
Stand back from the baggage carousel

The baggage carousel is where the mother of all bunching occurs. It's like all that other bunching throughout the trip was a mere rehearsal for the main event at the baggage carousel. People stand three and four rows deep around the carousel, pushing right up to the edge of it, making it difficult for anyone not in the front row to see their bag, let alone access it. If everyone would stand back a bit, then we would all be able to see and we would all be able to get in and out to retrieve our bags. And a note to parents, collecting the bags should not be viewed as a fun holiday activity for the whole family: move the kids back.

Appoint one designated bag collector and everyone else can stay out of the fray and act as spotters.

My dream is that airports will one day paint a thick yellow demarcation line around the carousel perimeter that creates a three-foot "no-standing zone" around the whole carousel. And it will be against the law to be caught standing inside that yellow line UNLESS you are physically removing your bag from the carousel.

SPECIAL SEALED SECTION
SCOOCHING

If you don't fly much, you can skip this next part; you have already suffered enough reading through my many rules about planes and airports. This section is specifically written for people who fly all the time and yet still don't understand how to move through the security check efficiently. The secret is scooching.

113
Scooch your bags right to the end
of the security conveyer belt

If I was shopping for a husband, I would go to the airport and watch people move through security. Anyone who gets it right is marriage material.

Heading into the security check, things aren't too bad; sometimes there's a bit of mild bunching, but overall it's a fairly orderly procedure. Passengers use the entire length of the conveyor belt and shuffle or "scooch" their stuff toward the X-ray machine.

Airside, however, everything grinds to a halt as passengers crowd the exit mouth of the X-ray machine, desperate to grab their items and start repacking their bags as soon as things emerge.

The flaw in the system is that people pass through the metal detector faster than bags pass through the X-ray. Add to that the complication that most people are waiting on more than one item. There's your bag, plus the laptop you removed from your bag, and there might be an aerosol and/or a belt in a separate tray. You might also have a little clear plastic bag of liquids and toiletries that you put in another tray and, depending on how aggressive—sorry "thorough"—the TSA is being that day, your shoes, watch, jewelry, and underpants might end up in another one. Potentially that's five trays for one person.

The solution to the multiple bags and trays, and the resulting pile-up of people hovering around the exit mouth of the X-ray, is scooching. You pass through the metal detector, take a brief turn at the exit mouth and scooch. No grabbing and repacking or sorting, just vigorously scooch any items that appear, be they yours or someone else's, scooch those mothers right down to the end of the conveyor belt. Then you can move yourself along the conveyor belt, out of the hot zone, and do all your repacking and re-belting business down at the far end. A little less grabbing and a bit more scooching would really help to keep things moving and prevent bunching.

ON THE ROAD

I don't suffer from road rage. That said, there's a good chance I incite a lot of it with my slow granny-style driving. I sit very close to the steering wheel and I rarely do the speed limit— twenty-five seems ample in a built-up area, and as for doing seventy on a freeway? Christ, I don't know if I could take the g-forces, I'm not Iceman in Top Gun.

The only time I become enraged on the road is when I allow a fellow motorist to cross into my lane or pull out into the flow of traffic and that person fails to raise a hand and tip me a thank-you wave. In that instance, it takes all my self-control not to follow that ignorant chucklehead home and sit outside their house with my hand stuck on the horn until they come out and acknowledge my magnanimous gesture. Which is why my first rule of the road is:

114
Courtesy waves are mandatory

When someone lets you in to traffic, acknowledge the act with a wave. Always. No exceptions. Courtesy breeds courtesy, and thank-you waves spread goodwill on the roads.

115
Courtesy waves from pedestrians are strongly encouraged

Yes, the law says that the driver must stop to allow you to cross at a pedestrian crossing, but that doesn't mean you shouldn't still give them a tip of the hat for doing so. I love a pedestrian who offers a smile and a nod to the driver as they cross, it's a real mood-lifter.

116
Be ready at the red light

Being first at the red light is a high-pressure position. And as such you must not do anything but stare at that red light and wait for it to change. No checking your makeup or your phone, don't start searching for a podcast or glancing at texts, just watch the red light. You need to be like a coiled spring, at the ready (riding the clutch if need be, keeping the car humming at friction point), so that the minute the light changes to green you can take off and allow as many cars as possible to get through that intersection. That's courteous driving.

117
Vacate the parking space if you can see someone is waiting

Don't be that person who pops their stuff in the trunk, jumps in the driver's seat, then sits there and doesn't leave despite the fact that someone else has pulled up alongside, put their blinker on, and is now holding up the traffic waiting for you to move on. If you can see a person waiting for the parking space, get out of there, don't start making calls or sending texts; you're not the Lincoln Lawyer, the car isn't your office, just drive off and relinquish the parking space.

118
It's a car, not a pencil case

No need to put stickers all over it. No one cares what radio station you listen to or that you shoot and vote, or that you have two stick-figure children, a stick-figure dog; and a stick-figure wife who likes surfing. No one cares that you shut the gate or lock the gate or whatever the latest thing is with gates and fracking. Most people *don't* support fracking, so really you should only need a sticker if you want to tell people you're really into it, maybe a sticker that says *Fracking! It's a gas gas gas!* or *My water is on fire! I heart fracking.*

119
Men don't look good driving convertible cars

There is simply no age where it looks right for a man to be driving a convertible car. If you're in your late teens/early twenties, you look like a spoiled child whose parents have bought you a convertible. If you're early thirties, you look like an investment banker who's bought the car as a personality proxy. If you're in your forties, you look like you're having a midlife crisis, and if you're any older than that you look like you've been told you have six months to live so you've chucked it all in and bought a convertible. Convertibles look better on women.

120
Parallel parking is not a spectator sport

Parallel parking is always a slightly tricky maneuver, but doing it in front of an audience—such as when you're parking outside a crowded cafe—increases the level of difficulty tenfold. Do the driver a courtesy and avert your eyes while they park. Do not, under any circumstances, settle into position, kick back, and watch the "show." It only makes the task harder and far less likely to happen in one neat attempt.

121
The horn is not a toy, use it sparingly

People who honk out of rage and frustration should be fined and their horn should be removed from their vehicle. I'm talking about those people who don't understand that holding your hand flat on the horn and honking it continually does not move the traffic forward. The red light can't hear you. And that traffic accident up ahead won't miraculously clear because you long-honked it.

The horn should only be used to deliver friendly reminders or alerts to fellow motorists. It's a way to say, "Hey buddy, light's gone green!" or "Yoohoo! I think you'll find traffic is on the move again." Or "Dude! Dude! Dude! Stop reversing, I'm right here behind you!" And the way you communicate those things is with a light touch. No pressing hard on the horn and making it wail like a bagpipe, that's not helping.

I would like to see horn-use included on the driving test. Before being awarded a license, the student driver should be required to demonstrate the various types of friendly honk, such as an amiable "toot toot," a light "parp," and, my favorite, a gentle "mip mip." Any flat-handed honking would be an immediate fail.

PUBLIC TRANSPORTATION

122
Don't sit next to someone unless there is no alternative

Basically this means that if you get on a bus or a train and there is a completely empty seat available, you are obligated to take that seat, even if you have to walk a bit further to get to it. Don't be a space invader and sit down to rub thighs with a stranger when there are still "full empties" available.

123
Headphones, headphones, headphones

This rule has already appeared in the plane travel section; however, it is also an important rule on every other form of public transportation.

124
Don't wait to be asked to move your bag off the seat

I don't mind people putting their bags on the seat next to them, sometimes it's just easier than putting them on the floor. But if the bus or train starts to fill up, don't be a dick, don't wait for someone to ask, just take your bags off the seat.

125
Stand up for old people

I love seeing an old person using public transportation. Not only does it mean they are keeping active and getting out and about but, better still, it means they are not behind the wheel of a car driving the wrong way around a roundabout or accelerating into cafes by accident. Let's encourage even more of them to get off the roads and onto public transportation by making sure it's always an easy and pleasant journey—and the way to do that is by standing up and offering them a seat.

126
The train is not your office

Some people like to get the jump on rush hour by quitting work early and then finishing the day's work on their cell phone during their commute home. This means everyone else on the train now has to endure your loud, tedious conversation about KPIs and ROIs and USP's. And FYI, we couldn't care less about any of it. So either don't leave work until you're finished, or if you must work on the train, do it via email. Not only is that something you can do quietly, but your colleagues are also far more likely to read an email than they are to listen to your self-important TPB (train phone blather).

127
Don't lean your whole body against the pole in the train vestibule

It makes it impossible for other standing passengers to hold onto the pole without groping you in unseemly places.

FOOD

GENERAL FOOD RULES

128
Avocado is a salad item

It doesn't belong in pasta. And it really doesn't belong in smoothies, what a waste of money. For an extra three bucks, all you're doing is adding a totally tasteless, pale green hue to your beverage and making it even more difficult to suck through a straw.

129
No tomato in guacamole

My book, my rules. And besides, tomato makes your guacamole watery and weird tasting.

130
Dark chocolate is not a treat

We all know this to be true. But for some reason health and "wellness" types refuse to admit it. They talk up dark chocolate like it's some kind of delicious sinful pleasure, always going on about how you only need "one square" as an after-dinner treat. Of course you only need one square, the stuff is bitter and unpleasant. Personally, I don't even want one square. Milk chocolate, however, I can poke that in my pie-hole row after delicious row!

131
Calling it "cacao" doesn't make it healthier than cocoa

You just moved a few letters around. Stop kidding yourself.

132
The only thing more disappointing than dark chocolate is carob

Except for the fact that they are both brown, carob is nothing like chocolate. As for being a good chocolate substitute, this is true only in the same way that sand is a good substitute for sugar. Giving carob to your children and telling them it's "yummy chocky" is tantamount to child abuse.

133
Don't get fancy with lettuce

Iceberg lettuce is crisp, it's crunchy, it's got enough structural integrity to hold up to a thick dressing and it's a terrific salad workhorse. You can throw in a few other leaves for decoration but if you're looking for a solid, crowd-pleasing base, go with iceberg.

134
A poke bowl is not a dumping ground for the contents of your fridge

Some people mistakenly think poke bowl means "poke whatever you can find into a bowl." Yes, the poke bowl is a convenient and easy way to make a meal, but you still need to pick some kind of theme for your melange of ingredients. Whether it's Asian, Italian, traditional Hawaiian, whatever, you must be consistent with your flavors. An example of something that is definitely not a poke bowl is this random set of ingredients: rice, spinach, tomato, three-bean mix, and satay-flavored tofu.

One of my fellow rule-makers witnessed that combination being "poked" together in a bowl by a colleague in the office kitchen. She was so horrified, she texted me to report it. She was (rightly) appalled by the disgusting mash-up of flavors.

I, too, was aghast; however, I was also intrigued by the mention of three-bean mix? I didn't even know you could still get that stuff? I thought it was like canned asparagus, just a distant and unpleasant-smelling memory from the 1970s.

135
You can't juice a guava

Don't believe the label that says "guava juice." There's nothing at all juicy about guavas. What you're really getting is a glass of thick, fibrous pink paste. Blergh.

136
Don't spend money on water

Doesn't matter how "artisanal" it is, or how pretty the shape or color of the bottle, it's still just water and you can get exactly the same thing out of the tap.

137
Keep your new food regime to yourself

Whether you've given up sugar or carbs or maybe you're fasting two days a week on the ol' 5-2, perhaps you're eating like a caveman or limiting your FODMAPs or your bibimbaps; whatever your new regime is, don't bang on about it. For, while I have nothing but respect for people who can be strict about their food intake, it's really boring when that's all they talk about.

I don't want to hear about your cheat days or your eight cups of green tea or your pale, straw-colored urine or your "delicious one square of dark chocolate" and I really don't want to be out to dinner with you when you grill the waitress about the ingredients and preparation method of every single dish on the menu.

138
Taste your meal before you salt it

This is a rule for old people who habitually reach for the salt and shake astonishing amounts of the stuff all over their food before they've even tasted it. Honestly, I could serve sea-water soup to my parents and they would still go at it with the salt. And I'm not saying you can't add salt, I'm saying you should do whoever has cooked the meal the courtesy of tasting it first, just one mouthful to consider the flavors and the subtle seasonings, then tip your salt all over it.

EATING

139
Eat like someone is watching

I don't care how you dance but you should always eat like someone is watching. People who live alone need to be particularly vigilant about this. When you eat on your own, there's no one to keep you in check and it's easy to get lazy. There's no one to look appalled when you use your fork like a shovel and hurl food into your mouth like coal into a locomotive steam engine. No one to shake their head gently and say, "too much, too much" when you try to poke a whole piece of sushi or roast potato into your mouth at once. Always eat with awareness to avoid developing bad habits that may shock others next time you are eating in company.

140
Don't overload your fork

If you can't get your forkful of food straight from the plate to your mouth without having to turn or rotate the fork in order to push everything into your mouth, then there's too much on it. Put your fork down, take a little bit off, and try again. There should be no complex maneuvering required. You're eating, not reverse parking food into your mouth.

141
Whatever goes in your mouth stays in your mouth

This rule tends to be abandoned when people eat spaghetti. We've all witnessed the human sausage grinder sitting across from us, with a long trail of spaghetti hanging out of their mouth that they bite off and let fall back into the bowl. Twirl it on your fork, people, twirl it on your fork, get all your strands secure, and then put it in your mouth. Or order penne. Especially if you're on a date; never order spaghetti, always request penne.

142
Don't order bucatini if you're hungry

Bucatini is that thick spaghetti pasta with a hole running through the center of it. It's an incredibly difficult pasta to manage because you can't suck it into your mouth like you can spaghetti and because it's so thick, it doesn't twirl easily around your fork. Plus the hole in the middle means you can't get any purchase. You can suck all you like but you're just pulling in air, it's like a pasta straw. All this makes for a very time-consuming meal, and I don't recommend it, especially if you're hungry.

143
No "smack-smacking"

Smack-smacking is a term that describes chewing with your mouth open. It pertains to the disgusting masticatory sound of food and saliva smacking together and then being amplified by the chewer's flapping gums. All you hear is "smack smack smack smack smack" echoing out of their gaping cake-hole.

This is another one of those rules that you wouldn't think needed to be written down. Just as Labradors are born knowing how to retrieve, surely humans should be born knowing that chewing with your mouth open is dizz-gusting.

144
No chipmunking

Chipmunking is the act of pushing food into the side of your mouth so you can talk with your mouth full. So-called because you look like a fat-faced little chipmunk when you do it—only a lot less adorable. I confess I break this rule a lot and need constant reprimanding. It must be genetic, because every member of my family is a chronic chipmunker. We love to eat and we love to talk and sometimes we find it hard to decide which of those things to prioritize.

145
Chew your food, don't inhale it

I have a tendency to get overexcited about food, which means I often eat too quickly. It's important to remember no one is coming to take your food. And it's not a race, there are no prizes for eating fast. If there are, then you should leave that establishment immediately. Eating contests are for idiots.

146
Sit down to eat

You can't enjoy your food while you're wandering around. Sit down. Eat properly. In parts of Japan they fine you for walking and eating, and if I have my way we'll soon introduce that law to the rest of the world as well.

147
"All you can eat" is not an order

It's not compulsory to eat as much as you can just because you're at an all-you-can-eat buffet. You are allowed to go to the buffet and simply eat what my mother would call "an elegant sufficiency." To be clear, I'm not exactly sure what that is but, if I had to guess, I'd say it means "Don't eat so much that you fall into a food coma."

148
"One plate only" is not a challenge

Some places offer an all-you-can-eat dining experience with the added restriction of one plate only. For Australians, this seems to encourage them to eat more than ever. They go at that buffet determined to make sure they don't get ripped off. This is why you see people carefully constructing Jenga-style towers of food, building their meal up in layers so as to fit as much as possible on their one plate. It's no longer about what they would like to eat, or how hungry they are, it's about getting their money's worth. But to what end? Yes, you're "screwing" the system, but you're also screwing your dining experience. Who can possibly enjoy a plate of mac and cheese flattened out by a chicken fried steak, topped with a layer of potato skins, then stacked with fourteen jumbo shrimp and finished off with a bunch of sketchy looking clams nestled on top. You may as well go and eat straight from the dumpster out the back.

Bonus Rule
If your food is too hot, stop eating it

We've all seen idiots do it. We've all been the idiot who does it. Whether it's a bowl of risotto with steam rising off it or a pizza straight out of the oven topped with molten lava-like cheese. You take a bite and instantly you know you've made a mistake. So you open your mouth and start huffing and talking while simulatenously trying to suck in air to cool down your food. "Ah ah ah, haht, haht, haht, hoo haht, hoo haht!" You wave your hand back and forth in front of your mouth and chew your food like a ventriloquist dummy laughing. Eventually you swallow it and say again, for anyone at the table who might have missed it, "oh my god, that food is so hot." Then what happens? You go straight back in and take another bite. For the love of god. Stop. Give it a minute to cool down. Let's earn our place at the top of the food chain.

DINING OUT

149
Lift your chair

Whether you're pulling it out to sit down or placing it back under the table when you leave, lift your chair. Don't drag it across the floor and make that hideous honking scraping sound: lift it. If you don't have the strength to lift your chair, perhaps you'd be better served at the gym than the cafe.

150
Be polite to servers

There is nothing more odious and embarrassing than being with someone who speaks rudely to servers. Also, you're playing with fire; think about it, they have access to your food, you don't know what they're going to do to it in the kitchen. Be nice.

151
Don't steal the pepper grinder

Obviously people do this and that's why cafes adopted the practice of having a single pepper grinder the size of a small child that the waiter brings to the table briefly and then swiftly removes. Please stop swiping the pepper grinders so we can all pepper our own food like grown-ups.

152
The waiter is not Judge Judy

So don't call them over and say "Settle an argument for us, would you ..."

153
Don't expect the chef to accommodate your food fad

Most restaurants post their menu online, so if you have a highly restrictive diet (by choice rather than because you have allergies) then check the menu first and, if it doesn't suit your new regime, don't go to that restaurant. Or maybe take a brief respite from your diet and enjoy a one-off meal with everything in it. Whatever you do, just don't ask the chef to change their signature dish to suit your dietary whims. That's rude. And so presumptuous. They run a restaurant, you came to them, they're not your personal chef.

154
Respect the non-drinker at the table

Make a mental note if someone is not drinking, and don't make them pay for alcohol. It's bad enough they have to stay sober and observe the rest of the table getting loose and starting to talk too loudly and make lame "jokes" with the waitstaff. Don't make them pay for the privilege as well. Being the only sober person at a table of drinkers is punishment enough.

155
Don't punish the vegetarian

If there is a vegetarian at a dinner where all the dishes are being shared, then either order plenty of vegetarian dishes for everyone to enjoy or lay off that one vegetarian dish at the table. It's galling for vegetarians to watch everyone hoeing into the only dish they can eat—and even more annoying when all the meat-eaters start going on about how delicious that one vegetarian dish is.

CAFES AND RESTAURANTS

156
Waiters, write it down

No one will think any less of you. Trust me when I say that nobody is impressed by the fact that you (apparently) are able to remember everything without writing it down. On the contrary, you're making everyone at the table feel tense. We're all sitting there thinking, *I bet he gets my order wrong.*

157
Don't hand out numbers on sticks

Nothing tempers your dining experience faster than finding out you have to order at the counter and then walk around the cafe wielding a number on a stick while you look for a table.

Ordering at the counter is particularly tricky for the single diner. When there are two people, one can hold the table while the other goes to order. But as the lonely lady diner, it's hard to claim a table until you've actually ordered. You have to either prematurely disrobe in order to leave an item of clothing draped across a chair, or remove something not particularly valuable from your bag and deposit that on the table. Something like a book or a pair of spectacles (but it can't be a Kindle or sunglasses because someone might steal those things). I don't always carry a bag so I've been left in the unfortunate position of trying to stake a claim on a table by leaving the contents of my pocket on it—a lip gloss, a pen, and a dirty tissue. If you don't do this and the cafe is crowded, then you run the risk of having nowhere to sit and eat the food you've just ordered and paid for.

158
Jokes on cafe chalkboards do not bring in clientele

It's the promise of good coffee that draws people into a cafe, not a pithy gag on a chalkboard, like this one I saw recently: *My friend told me I was delusional. I nearly fell off my unicorn!* Hmm, perhaps if they were a better friend, they'd have told you not to write those words on a chalkboard outside your cafe. The problem is, these things are mildly amusing the first time you read them but you need to commit to a new one every day, otherwise you just annoy people. I have walked past this particular gem half a dozen times in the last week—*Jesus was a Carpenter but he didn't sing on any of the albums*—and it's starting to feel like I'm at a party standing with a drunk person who keeps telling me the same unfunny story again and again. Why not just write something that will stand the test of time and be appreciated every day like, *Come on in, we don't charge four dollars for a latte!*

159
No communal dishes of sea salt

Sure, that miniature bowl containing a mound of salt (that everyone is dipping their grubby fingers into) looks aesthetically pleasing, but in reality it is a potpourri of pathogens. I know specialty salt is all the rage now, with many varieties like truffle salt and lemon myrtle salt, but I think we can all agree to live without bacteria salt. Bring back the saltshaker.

160
No vegetables in the coffee

The Pumpkin Pie Spice Latte is the vegemite of the United States. Some people love it, some people love to hate it. I have no objection to whatever combination of spices you want to put in your coffee, but I draw the line at adding actual pumpkin puree. Which, I'm reliably informed, is the latest ingredient for an "authentic" pumpkin spice latte. Once you start stirring mashed pumpkin into your coffee, it stops being a seasonal novelty beverage and becomes something you'd blend up for Grandad when he can't find his teeth but still insists on having a piece of pie with his coffee.

161
Talk and froth people, talk and froth

No one minds a chatty barista. It can be nice to stand at the counter and shoot the breeze. Baristas tend to be excellent at driving small talk and I'm into it. Unless it's busy. In which case, let's either keep chitchat to a minimum or continue the confab *while* you pull those shots and froth that milk. But don't stop frothing in order to chat, that makes everyone antsy.

In return, I would ask customers to respect your busy periods by limiting their coffee orders to three. We've all stood in line thinking there was just enough time to grab a coffee and still make it back to work without being late. Only to have the person in front of us step up and start rattling off the entire office's coffee order. Three coffees max during busy times. Let's keep the country moving.

162
Don't try to guess my income, just bring tapwater

Being asked "Do you want still or sparkling water?" as soon as you sit down at a restaurant feels like a rather unsubtle way of asking whether the customer is cashed up or a cheapskate. Restaurants should assume that everyone wants water and simply bring tap water to the table on arrival.

If the customer is appalled by the idea of drinking water from a tap, they will no doubt make it known and request some overpriced bottled still water. Same goes for sparkling water. If someone wants it, they'll ask for it. No one has ever sat in a restaurant thinking, *Hmm, they haven't mentioned sparkling water ... they probably don't have it, best not to make a fool of myself by asking for it.*

163
If the avocado is hard as a rock, don't serve it

And don't even think about charging three bucks extra for it as a side order.

164
Don't serve food on planks, tiles, slabs of granite, or any other building materials

Bowls and plates are more than adequate. If in doubt as to whether a vessel is suitable for food service, check that there is some kind of lip or edge to it—you need enough to keep your food from constantly falling off onto the table and to stop any food from shooting across at the diner opposite you should your knife or fork slip.

165
Leave room between tables for a standard-sized caboose

It's never enjoyable when cafes put tables too close together. It's humiliating to have to slide your bum across the next table's eating surface whenever you squeeze yourself in or out.

166
Tip jar gags reduce your chances of getting a tip

It's best to play it safe and simply write *TIPS* on the tip jar. Not *Staff Retirement Fund, Give Generously—Winky face* or *Tip It, Tip It Good!* or *If you fear change, leave it with us!* And under no circumstances should you sex-shame your patrons at the counter: *Generous tippers make generous lovers.* Eww.

167
Enforce the "Please wait to be seated" sign

I'm a big fan of cafes and restaurants that like to control the flow of customers into their establishment. I love an orderly system and I love it when there's no ambiguity as to what the system is, which is why I like it when I see a *Please wait to be seated* sign. However, if you are going to make such a bold claim about having a system, then someone must be on hand to implement that system. You need a designated greeter. Without a greeter keeping tabs on arrivals and doing the job of greeting and seating, what happens is the obedient people like myself stand at the entrance for ages, like dolts, while flagrant rule-breakers barge past and claim all the tables. You can't rely on your regular waitstaff to fill the greet-and-seat role because the minute they get busy, they will suddenly develop "waiter vision impairment syndrome," which is when they pretend they can't see you or anyone else in the queue of well-behaved patrons standing patiently at the door.

168
Don't make me curate my own lunch

At lunchtime, everyone is in a hurry. No one has the time to stand at the counter and choose a base and then a protein and then a "crunch" plus one optional extra topping for free and any further toppings for a dollar each (except for avocado, that's two dollars) plus a dressing. You lost me at step two of your five-step process, I've just walked next door to order the number 12 sandwich.

169
Put the parmesan cheese down and walk away

Leave it at the table. Don't dole it out in polite but insufficient quantities or make me feel like a cheese-pig by calling you back three times to get some more. Just leave it at the table. Let me be in charge of the cheese.

SPECIAL SEALED SECTION
FRUIT

You might think this is going to be a section where I upbraid people for not categorizing their fruits and vegetables correctly. However, I actually find that whole fruit vs. vegetable thing rather tedious. Certain people delight in shouting you down for calling a tomato a vegetable. "It's a fruit! The tomato is a fruit! It has seeds! It's a fruit!" These are the same people who can't wait to tell you that the peanut is a legume and that the potato is a deadly nightshade. Yawn. Who cares? As far as I'm concerned, there are far more important rules about fruit.

170
Fruit is not dessert

This is actually my sister's rule. She is forever disappointed when someone offers fruit for dessert. She maintains that fruit can only be categorized as dessert if it is sprinkled with sugar and served with ice cream. Another friend of mine goes further and insists fruit is only dessert if it is smothered in custard. And then there's my mother who thinks that a single, plain, unadorned piece of fruit is the *only* way to finish a meal. I'm somewhere in between these two camps when it comes to fruit. For me, it all comes down to selection and preparation.

171
No filler fruits in fruit salad

Fruit salad can be absolutely delicious; however, all too often it is spoiled by the inclusion of what I call "filler fruits." Things like oranges and apples and, god forbid, banana. These are clearly stand-alone fruits, they are supposed to be consumed as a single piece; they're not for cutting up and throwing into the salad melange. Especially banana. The strong flavor of a banana permeates the whole salad and makes everything taste of banana; it also has an unpleasant mucilaginous quality that coats all the other fruits with brownish slime. Apple is also problematic because it goes brown and looks unpalatable within half an hour. And too many people cut up bits of orange without properly removing the pith, so you have to suffer all that white, leathery stuff on every piece. The easiest solution is to leave these fruits out of the fruit salad.

172
The fruit salad in the display cabinet is a mirage

We've all stood at the shop counter and been fooled by the delicious-looking tray of fruit salad. There's a whole healthy mountain of fruity goodness piled high (apparently) with strawberries and watermelon and passionfruit and all the top-shelf fruits that you actually enjoy eating, like blueberries and sometimes even mango. Yet when the man behind the counter reaches in with his big silver spoon and shovels out your serving, somehow you don't get any of that top layer; you end up with what lies beneath—those sad, pastel chunks of unripe cantaloupe and honeydew melon, and occasionally a few anemic cubes of fibrous, tasteless pineapple—and if it's a really shitty place, no doubt there'll also be a fair share of those filler fruits I mentioned in the previous rule.

If you're lucky you might get one or two slivers of strawberry, but that's it. Turns out those "whole" strawberries on the top are a complete trompe l'oeil, placed there to lure you in. The rest of the strawberries in the salad (all four of them) have been carefully shaved into about half a dozen wafer-thin slices and sprinkled parsimoniously throughout.

173
There is a right way to cut up an orange

Oranges were the original team snack for kids playing sports. Each week at games across the land, one kid's mom would be tasked with bringing a Tupperware box of cut-up oranges and handing them round to the hot sweaty kids at half-time. I don't know who invented that tradition, I'm guessing some smart farmer from orange-growing country. At our basketball games, we'd suck on an orange quarter while the coach reminded us to use everyone on the team, not just Lauren Fraser. Lauren was easily the best player, but that wasn't why we passed her the ball. We did it because she'd get really red in the face and yell at you if you didn't. People always think it must be hard for kids who aren't good at sports. I think it must be harder for kids who are good at it—they're the ones who would be winning every week if only they weren't on teams full of useless kids who constantly let them down. Sorry, Lauren.

Orange duty was rotated around the mothers, so my own mom only had to do it once every eight weeks. And that was a shame, because she was the only one who knew the right way to cut up an orange, and I think that's because she invented it. I implored her to tell the other mothers how to do it, but she was either too smart to do something as dumb as tell another mother how to cut up fruit, or she just didn't care. Maybe a bit of both. My mom wasn't big on watching a bunch of uncoordinated idiots (and one Lauren) run around a basketball court. And who can blame her?

For anyone who wants to know the right way to cut up an orange, I have included a diagram of my mother's simple technique. It guarantees six perfect segments of orange with not a scrap of pith on any piece. Because nobody likes the "yucky white bit."

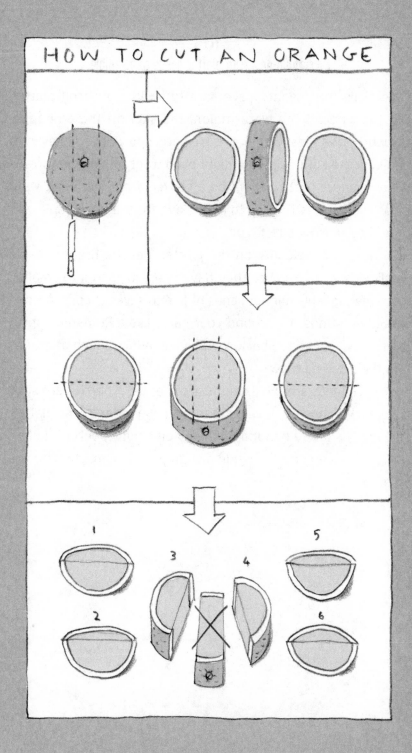

174
Everything on a fruit platter needs to be edible

Essentially this means: make an effort with your fruit platter. Cut the rind off the watermelon, the skin off the pineapple (*properly*, don't leave any of those hard, spiky brown eyes in it) and peel the kiwi fruit; you might even want to hull your straw-berries before putting them on a platter. What you don't want is for your guests to have to go looking for the trash can every time they finish a bit of fruit.

Grapes are welcome on the platter, despite the inevitable "stalk waste." Make sure they have been snipped into smaller, more manageable mini-bunches of five to seven grapes. No one should be wandering around your party like a Roman emperor at an orgy, head tilted back, lowering an entire bunch of grapes into their gaping maw.

And cherries are the exception to the rule. Cherries are such a treat, everyone will love you for including them on the platter. I'll happily shove a handful of cherry pits in my pocket if I can't find a trash can or a little side dish to put them in, cherries are so great!

RELATIONSHIPS & DATING

A Word about Mixed Messages

A friend of mine set me up with a man once. The man was the brother of my friend's friend, which is a good degree of separation for matchmaking. You never want it to be too close to home in case it goes wrong. I know some people hate the idea of a setup but I'm all for it; after all, who knows you better than your friends and family? Surely being set up by a friend makes more sense than online dating or going out to public places and sitting in the corner looking hopeful. And at the time this setup occurred, I'd been single for so long I was even contemplating asking my mom if any of her friends had sons whose marriages were on the rocks and looked likely to be coming back on the market.

According to my friend, this man—let's call him George (even though his name was Ben)—was just my type. And as it turned out, my friend was right. "George" was really nice— he was smart and funny and attractive. We went out, had a couple of drinks, the conversation was interesting and easy, and I was thinking, Well, this is just perfect, what a great couple we make, and we already have mutual friends! I can't wait for us all to get together and have dinner and laugh about why this never happened sooner! Why are people so weird about being set up? George and I are perfect for each other. I wonder when we'll get married . . .

There was only one tiny thing wrong with George and that was that he didn't feel the same way about me. I can't imagine why not. I mean, I'm so easygoing, it's not like I have 488 rules about everything from fruit to flatulation. I guess I just wasn't his cup of tea. Unfortunately, George was also very polite, so I had no clue that I wasn't his cup of tea.

After our hugely successful (I thought) first date, I texted him and suggested another date; he said he was busy but maybe another time, so I texted again. And again. And by the third "I'm a bit busy at the moment," the penny finally dropped and I realized he wasn't interested. Actually, maybe I didn't. Now that I think about it, I'm pretty sure my friend had to tell me George wasn't interested. Poor George must have called his sister and said, "Hey, can you tell your friend to tell his friend to back off, she keeps texting me and I'm clearly not interested!" The message was passed along and by the time it got to me, I think it had been diluted a bit so as not to totally crush my feelings. I imagine it started out as, "Jesus, tell that idiot to take a hint, I don't want to go on another date!" to "Um . . . he's very busy at work and doesn't have time for a relationship right now" to "I'm pretty sure he just broke up with someone and he's not in the right headspace at the moment." In the end, they all mean the same thing: "He's not interested." And sure, my pride was a little hurt, but sometimes a reality check can be useful—it's not a bad thing to realize that not everyone thinks you're the bee's knees.

Over a year later, I got a text from George telling me that he'd just seen me on some comedy gala on TV and had really enjoyed my work. He was very complimentary and he signed off the text with an "x." I showed it to my friend who immediately said, "You should text him, maybe he's in the right headspace now." And so, like an idiot, I did. I texted and suggested we go for a drink, and guess what? George said yes! We set a date for the following week. The night before our date, George texted to say something had come up and asked if we could reschedule. I said "sure" and we set another date. Then, a few days later, he texted to ask if we could raincheck again to the following week. This time I called him because I felt emboldened and like I wanted to be insulted in person rather than just via text. "Hello, George," I said (even though his name was Ben). "It's Kitty here. Listen, do you want to just cancel and forget this whole thing?"

If I'm being completely honest, I thought he would apologize profusely and say, "No, no, no, I really want to do this, I'm just having trouble finding a free night," but he didn't. He sounded extremely relieved and said, "Yes! I'm sorry, do you mind? I don't know why I said yes in the first place." Now I don't mind if someone doesn't want to go out with me, but if you're not interested, then my advice would be don't send me complimentary texts out of the blue and definitely don't sign those texts with an "x." In fact, the next time you see me on the telly and think I'm funny, maybe just think it, don't text it. I guess if there was a rule here, it would be, don't send x's to someone you have no interest in x'ing.

FIRST DATE DON'TS

Most people are very wary on first dates, always on the lookout for what's wrong with the other person—after all, there must be a reason they are still single. The exception is childless women between 35 and 43—this demographic is absurdly positive and willing to see the good in anyone because they sense their fertility window closing, and that makes them a whole lot less particular about potential mates. For the rest of us, however, any transgression, no matter how small, is usually enough to kibosh the possibility of a second date, which is why you need to be on your absolute best behavior on that first outing. Here are some things to avoid if you are hoping to score that elusive second date.

175
One to two squirts max of perfume or aftershave

You don't want your date to smell you before they see you. Be it perfume, aftershave, or Axe body spray, one squirt is ample, two is okay, but you're pushing it. And if it happens to be the perfume Angel by Thierry Mugler, then no squirts at all is preferable. That stuff is like a biological weapon—even a single squirt is enough to render me nauseous and two squirts has me reaching for a gas mask.

176
Men, don't wear the whale tail or shark tooth necklace

Best to wait a few months until you've really hooked her with your sweet personality and sense of humor, then hopefully she'll find it within herself to forgive your awful man jewelry.

177
Don't be late

Nothing says your time is less valuable than mine like turning up late. On a first date, you can at least afford this new person the courtesy of being on time.

Texting that you're going to be late is still being late—your lateness is not excused because you forewarned the person of your impending lateness. Be on time.

178
Don't mention your ex

There's no good way to talk about your ex on a first date. If you are nice and positive about them, you will sound like you're still in love with them. And if you trash-talk them, you will sound like you're a bit unhinged . . . and you're still in love with them.

179
Don't show pictures of your kids

It's too early for that. You may show pictures of your dog (as long as the dog is not wearing an outfit of any kind). And men may show pictures of their cat; however, for the ladies, while you can admit to owning a cat, you should hold off on showing any pictures of it on a first date. I know that's sexist, but I'm afraid I only make the rules, not society's attitudes.

180
Don't perform a monologue, have a conversation

A conversation is a "turn-take" arrangement: you talk, then the other person talks. There should be at least two voices participating in a conversation. Don't relegate your date to being an audient for your monologue or your well-rehearsed "life highlights" package (see Conversation Rules for further clarification).

181
Don't go for dinner

I don't recommend going for dinner on a first date—there are way too many rules to think about when you're eating. Best to keep it simple and just go for a drink. Or see a movie. The movie date is an excellent first date because not only does it give you something to talk about afterward, but it also allows you to see how the other person behaves in the movie theater: you will find out immediately whether they know the rules of moviegoing.

182
Don't eat the nuts or pretzels

If the date is going well and you decide you like the person, then avoid snacking from the bowl of nuts or pretzels on the bar. No one wants to kiss someone with nut breath or chewed-up nut paste in their teeth. And pretzels are just as bad—they really get stuck in your teeth and, on top of that, they make your breath smell like pee.

COUPLES

183
No love on the escalator

The escalator is a thoroughfare, please don't clog it up with your public demonstrations of affection. Couples who stand side-by-side holding hands are the worst. Never ever stand two abreast. Even if you really really love your new boyfriend or girlfriend, give it a rest for the duration of the escalator ride. Stand one behind the other but resist the urge to turn yourselves into a love sculpture. Shopping malls are rife with young lovers taking advantage of the free stair ride to caress one another. Remember, it's only a temporary separation, you'll be next to one another again in less than a minute. And if you really can't take being apart for that long, then end your separation sooner by walking up or down the escalator. That's how you're supposed to use the escalator, by the way; they were designed to *assist* your journey, you're not supposed to become a human statue the minute you hit one.

184
Grocery shopping is not a romantic activity

Newly loved-up couples enjoy spending every minute together. For some young women, going to the supermarket is often a chance to play house, dragging their man through the aisles, pushing the cart together, and fondling each other in front of the Cheerios as they attempt to conjure up some kind of cutesy faux-domesticity before the relationship has reached that level of familiarity. But kids, slow down, there's really no need to rush into such mundane routine behavior—your relationship will get there soon enough and there won't be anything cutesy about it. Leave yourself somewhere to go, don't peak too early!

If you're holding hands in the supermarket, you should be at home. You're obviously still in those early stages where you're not even hungry anyway. So go home. Have sex. Order takeout.

185
Wait at least six months before giving each other pet names

Preferably longer. There is nothing worse than someone going too early with the pet name, no matter what that pet name might be: honey, muffin, darling, love, pumpkin, sweetheart, or, god forbid, "babes." The same goes for referring to one another as your boyfriend or girlfriend—I like to wait at least two years before I use that term, going any earlier feels like you're tempting fate.

186
Don't use the word "lover"

It's too visual. Now we're all imagining you guys doing it. Ew.

187
No emojis when texting your partner

This is a rule I instigate when I am in a relationship. I find the use of emojis to be an extremely lazy form of communication, and I think when it comes to your partner you should make an effort and do more than just "thumbs up" them or "smiley winky face" them. I am well aware that a lot of people will now be "crying laughy face-ing" me and thinking, *Well, no wonder you're not in a relationship, lady!* And to those people I say "poo with eyes" to you.

See, I'm not banning the use of emojis when texting, just when texting your partner. They're supposedly the most important person in your life, so take the time to write out what you actually mean, even if it's just the actual words "thumbs up, see you later." It takes a few seconds longer, but it says you care and it's also mildly amusing, which is never a bad thing.

188
Never propose to someone in public

It puts way too much pressure on the other person to say yes.

189
If someone proposes in public, say yes even if you don't mean it

It's the kind thing to do. Later on, in private, you can take your "yes" back and explain that you didn't want to embarrass them in public by saying no.

190
Don't fart in front of your partner

I know this is contentious. People say it's a sign of being relaxed and comfortable with your partner if you can really be yourself and, quite literally, let go in front of them. But ask yourself a few questions: Did you fart in front of them on the first date when you were trying to be impressive and sexy? Do you fart openly at work? Or at the shops? Or in restaurants? I say "openly" because I know everyone farts; I mean, who hasn't accidentally blown off at the Hobby Lobby counter while buying dressmaking scissors? My point is, there's a difference between sneaking one out (or being caught completely off guard by a relaxed sphincter muscle at Hobby Lobby), and intentionally lifting your cheek and letting one rip in front of the person you, apparently, love above all others. Surely that person deserves the same amount of respect that you offer people such as work colleagues, servers, and shopkeeps. Familiarity breeds contempt.

191
Don't pick your nose in front of your partner

As above. A little bit of subtle digital inquiry around the edges of the nostrils is okay occasionally, but don't be plunging that finger up to the knuckle and rummaging so hard you risk punching through to your eyeballs. I'm not saying you can't pick your nose, just do it in private.

192
Never use the phrase "Happy wife, happy life"

This phrase tends to be uttered by men who can't be bothered to communicate with their partners. It's their way of saying, "Yeah fine, whatever." It's their way of keeping the old "ball and chain" happy. And by keeping her happy, I mean quiet. Apparently they prefer to just nod and go along with whatever is said rather than actually listen to a woman's concerns and potentially have a spirited discussion about the issue.

193
Declare immediately that your partner is in the car with you when you answer the phone

The minute you press that speakerphone button, you must declare not only that you are in the car but that there are others present. Before the caller has a chance to speak, jump right in with: "Hello! I'm in the car with Pete, say hello to Pete because he is right here next to me and he can hear you because we are on speakerphone, in the car, together. Pete can hear you, and I can hear you, we can both hear you . . . so, go ahead please, caller."

194
Don't have a shared email address with your partner

Grow up, guys. You are two individual people. And I should be able to write to my friend without having to worry that their spouse could also be reading my embarrassing, overthinking, girly missives.

Bonus Rule
Gentlemen, when you don't know something, admit it

The only thing sexier than a man who can admit he doesn't know something is a man who can say: "Oh, I'm sorry, I was wrong." That's how you talk a lady into bed right there. Oh, and cleaning the kitchen helps, too.

FRIENDS OF COUPLES

195
Don't go too early with your opinion when a couple breaks up

Always wait for the couple to break up, get back together, then break up again before revealing how you really feel about the ex-partner.

ONLINE DATING RULES—FOR MEN

196
Don't list loving your kids as an attribute

This rule is really directed at divorced dads who are dating again. Tell your kids you love them by all means, as often as you like, but there's no need to tell someone you just met by dropping it into your dating profile as if it's a personality trait or a hobby. "Hi, I'm Devon, I'm 46, I work at Macquarie Bank, I enjoy stand-up paddle boarding and I really love my kids." These men seem to think that "loving their kids" makes them especially great guys. But it doesn't. Loving your kids is completely normal. Of course you love your kids, you're genetically predisposed to love them, there's no need to mention it. In fact, you should love them so much that you refuse to use them as date bait. On the other hand, if you *don't* love your kids, then by all means drop that into the mix because that's completely unexpected and definitely worth discussing.

197
Don't compare yourself to James Bond

Online dating isn't supposed to be all about looks. Unlike apps such as Tinder, which are based almost exclusively on appearance, many of the dating websites purport to be less superficial, offering a chance to find out more about a person by reading their comprehensive written profile. And that's why your username is so important.

The username says a lot about you. Any woman who has tried online dating has no doubt come across countless '007s, whether it's "Phil007" or "IanB007." There are also plenty of '69s—guys who like to add the suffix 69 to their username, perhaps because they were born in 1969 or more likely to let the ladies know that they are really into blow jobs. Sweet. Good to know, guys.

Obviously I'm not Beyoncé and I don't speak for all the single ladies, but I would like to meet someone who puts a bit more thought into their username. Someone who takes a moment to come up with something pithy or at least mildly amusing, like SmokedMeatEnthusiast or CondimentMan.

Spend your creative energy coming up with a good username and don't bother filling out the rest—no one cares that your favorite movie is *The Shawshank Redemption,* and it's news to nobody that you enjoy good food. Who doesn't like good food?

198
Use a normal photo of yourself

The best way to explain normal is by defining "not normal." For example:

A photo of yourself, standing shirtless in the bathroom holding your phone up to the mirror—that's not normal. You think you're showcasing your fabulous body and tempting all the laydeez with your abs, but in reality what most women see is a self-obsessed guy who takes photos of himself in the mirror.

A selection of pictures of you standing next to world-famous landmarks—that's not normal. You think it makes you look like a well-traveled gent, but in reality it makes you look like a lonely guy who went on a Contiki tour.

A photo of you wearing a suit at a wedding with a woman who has been cropped out of the photo but not completely— that's not normal. You think that by leaving just enough of her in the photo, women will note that you have dated attractive women before, which will increase your chances with other attractive women. In reality, this photo sends the subliminal message that you are a psychopath who chops things up when his girlfriend leaves him. Maybe it's just the photo of the girlfriend you chopped up or maybe it's actually the girlfriend and she's now in pieces in your freezer. I'm not saying that's what you've done, I'm just saying that's where our minds go when we see a photo of a man with a dismembered lady's arm draped across his shoulders.

The *normal* thing to do is ask a friend to take a decent head-and-shoulders shot of you.

ONLINE DATING RULES—FOR WOMEN

199
Use a current photo

That's the most important rule. Don't use a photo that is ten years old. Or heavily filtered (unless you can filter your face in real life as well). And maybe don't have a photo of yourself jumping in the air. The number of women on dating websites who have a photo of themselves jumping into the air like they're doing a Toyota commercial leads me to believe that women have a peculiar idea of what men are looking for. I've yet to meet a man who says to me: "Hey lady, you look nice, but before we go for a drink, answer me this: what's your vertical leap like? Seriously, how high can you jump, from a standing start?"

200
Don't waste time filling out a profile

It's pointless, no man is ever going to do anything but look at your photo. If you must write something in the profile section, just say that you do yoga. For some reason, men think women who do yoga are going to be super-flexible and totally up for being bent over tables and contorted into all manner of weird sex-pretzel shapes.

SEX

201
If you're going to make porn, get paid for it

The internet is almost full and ninety percent of the content is amateur porn. It's one of life's great mysteries that there are so many people out there who make videos of themselves having sex then upload it for everyone to watch. For free.

I would implore people to stop doing this. If I want to see plain doughy people having sex, I'll put a mirror on my ceiling.

202
Always take your shoes off before trying to remove jeans or pants

No matter how urgent you are to be nude, taking your shoes off first will always save you time in the long run.

203
If you tell people you are a sex therapist, expect to have to talk about it

Putting aside the fact that this job seems a bit suspect and sounds like the modern-day equivalent of those guys in the seventies who walked around wearing T-shirts that said *Sex Instructor, first lesson free!*, let's accept that sex therapist is a legitimate job. And in return, sex therapists must accept that when people discover there's a sex therapist at the dinner table, that is all anyone is going to want to talk about. No one is going to shrug and say, "Sure, whatever, sounds dull, let's talk to Nathan, he's an actuary!" It's a bit like being a midwife—some jobs are just interesting. The difference is midwives (and nurses) usually tend to be very generous with their work stories.

Not so the sex therapist. I was at dinner once with someone who happened to be a sex therapist, and she got a bit huffy when we all took a gleeful interest in finding out exactly what her "job" entailed, all of us peppering her with questions: "Do you have to have sex with the person? Or do you just talk about sex?" "Or do you watch that person having sex with someone else and call out encouragement from the sidelines like a coach?" "What qualifications do you need? Is there an exam?" But instead of regaling us with fascinating tales of women whose vaginas clamp shut or men with knobs shaped like baseball bats, she looked rather put-upon, rolled her eyes, and said, "Why does everyone always want to talk about my job?"

Oh please, why do you think? Stop pretending it's not intriguing and that we should just take it in our stride. If you don't want to talk about it, don't mention it; next time, tell people you are a life coach and we'll all happily leave you alone.

204
Being a sex addict is not a thing

Sex addicts only ever seem to be "diagnosed" as such once they are busted having an affair or affairs. Until they are caught, they are just a regular person being unfaithful to their partner. But once the partner finds out about it, suddenly it's a disease and they can't help themselves. Curious.

205
Keep it down if you know there are people within earshot

It's quite possible to have sex quietly; you don't have to broadcast your good times, especially if it's two in the morning and you're in a hotel with paper-thin walls. Have some consideration for the lonely traveler in the next room.

206
Don't refer to sex as "being intimate" with someone

Please.

Bonus Rule
Sex is like gumbo, it doesn't have to be spicy

At some stage in a relationship, one person invariably suggests "spicing things up in the bedroom." And for some reason, this always seems to involve putting something "on you," whether it's whipped cream or fluffy handcuffs or, God forbid, the freakin' neighbor. Humans are the only species who feel the need to get kooky in the bedroom. You never see wildlife documentaries about the deviant male hippo in the herd who likes to suck the pretty girl hippos' toes. And it's a well-known fact that giraffes don't ever have to negotiate a safe word before they get down to it. Maybe a little more focus on good technique and a little less focus on spicy props is in order.

PARENTING

A Word about the Parenting Expert

*As a childless person, or barren spinster (my preferred nomenclature), you might wonder what sort of qualifications I have to dole out parenting advice, let alone lay down actual rules for parenting. I would say that the very reason I am able to give such great advice is **because** I am childless. You see, I'm still a purist, an idealist. I have not got parenting wrong, I have not been defeated or worn down, I remain unsullied by the real-life experience of having children. That's why I'm able to tell all you parents how great it could be, if only you followed the rules.*

GENERAL PARENTING RULES

207
Don't name your child after an inanimate object

Banjo. Blanket. Candlestick.

Verbs don't necessarily make great names either: Dream. Reign. Skip. Blanch. Mash.

And you should definitely think twice before you name your child after cheese: Cheddar. Wensleydale. Buffalo Mozzarella. Even Brie only works if you can guarantee the kid is going to grow up to be really, really good looking.

208
Birth videos should only be viewed by the people who made the baby

Film the birth of your child if you must, but don't have a screening for your friends, no matter how dear those friends are. And definitely don't horrify your other children by showing it to them either. Sure, childbirth is a beautiful, amazing, natural thing, but no one needs to bear witness to exactly how wide that hole can go.

209
It's not babysitting if they are your children

This is a common bugbear for a lot of mothers. For some reason, fathers will often refer to staying home to look after their own children as "babysitting," as if it's some sort of chore rather than an inherent part of being a parent.

210
Do not negotiate with children

When you give in to a child's demands, it creates a precedent and guarantees more hijackings of family outings and even more insane demands in future.

211
Boobs yes, Bugaboos no

Breastfeeding mothers, you are welcome in cafes, restaurants, kiosks; wherever you want to get your nourishers out is absolutely fine. Nobody cares. If we're staring at you, it's only because we're trying to work out the right way to salute you for being such amazing people and giving life to a new generation. We don't even care if you bring your toddler into the cafe and spend a stupid amount of money on a teeny-tiny cup of frothy milk that your child adoringly refers to as a "bubbycheemo" (oh bless). Points to you for keeping the economy buoyant.

The thing people object to about mothers in cafes is when you gather en masse and choke the place up with a cluster of those giant Bugaboo strollers. Like you're a bunch of cowboys circlin' the wagons and gittin' ready for a shoot-out. Two strollers max inside per group. Even then, one is preferable. Spare a thought for the poor servers who have to negotiate their way around these hazards while carrying hot beverages. If the group has multiple strollers, why not get to-go coffees and go to the park instead? Kids prefer the park, they really do.

212
Your child's snot is your responsibility

When you see it, wipe it. Without delay. During the early years, your child is still a strange hybrid creature, half human/half petri dish. But you can't expect a child to care about having what is essentially an opencut mine of disease streaming out of their nostrils. That's why you, as the parent, are responsible for whisking that snot away as quickly as possible before it can be transferred onto anyone or anything else.

213
No bare bums on tables

It is, of course, an absolute outrage when a cafe doesn't provide a changing table in the bathroom and you should definitely take that up with management or perhaps call *Sixty Minutes* and have them send a reporter in to badger the owner aggressively about why they hate children and why they think mothers are second-class citizens who don't deserve equal rights. But just because the cafe is disrespecting you by not having a changing table, it doesn't mean you have the right to punish all the other innocent diners with the sight of your child's butthole being lifted and wiped on a table right next to where they are eating.

214
Childless people reserve the right to be both petrified of and disgusted by lice

As a parent, you are obliged to deal with these revolting and terrifying parasites in a rational and non-alarmist fashion. It's your job, it's what you signed up to do when you had a kid. In return you receive unconditional love from your child and, if you play your cards right, someone to look after you when you get old and infirm.

Childless people receive none of these benefits or rewards, which is why we are compensated by living in a world without small creatures that bring home even smaller microscopic creatures crawling all over them. So don't roll your eyes and "tsk" at us when we freak out and refuse to come over to your place when your kid has lice. Or worms. Or school sores. Or whooping cough and measles if you live in Clark County, Oregon—which, considering the low vaccination rate, should really think about changing its name to Ground Zero.

215
Don't put your child on the phone to "say hello"

Children are not great on the phone; if you work hard enough you can extract a few single-word answers from them, but most of the time you just listen to them huff and breathe into the phone like a creepy stalker. Even when you are the child's owner it can be hard to get more than a few words out of them. I've heard many people struggling to keep a "conversation" going with their own child but I guess, as a parent, you don't mind so much because you simply enjoy hearing every precious breath your child takes. But for the rest of us, we've got stuff we could be getting on with. The exception, of course, is Grandma. If I was a parent, I'd make calling Grandma a daily event, I'd say a quick hello then whack my kid on the phone with Grammy while I hustled off to get a few jobs done. Old person and young child on the phone are like peanut butter and jelly—the perfect combination; one likes to prattle on and the other just makes an occasional breathing noise to assure you that there is actually someone "listening" at the other end.

216
Reserve the phrase "good job" for something worthwhile

Children get accolades for the most basic of tasks these days. When they sit down at the dinner table it's "good job, sweetie." If they flush the toilet it's "good job, Tilly." Even the act of taking their cup to the sink elicits a "good job, Xander." I'm worried this might make life difficult for children when they get older and enter the workforce. All this "good-jobbing" could make them confused and needy. I imagine they'll be sitting at their desk on their first day wondering why a coworker didn't say "good job" for drinking their coffee without spilling it or why the boss hasn't "good-jobbed" them for arriving on time and sitting up straight. Let's reward them with "good job" when they do something genuinely useful, like mow the lawn or retile the bathroom.

217
Don't climb Mount Everest if you have children under eighteen

When you have children, you are obliged to try to stay alive for them at least until they reach adulthood. Climbing Mount Everest is a pointlessly dangerous endeavor. I say pointless because it's not a mountain that needs to be conquered. It's already been conquered. Many times over. And filing up the mountain in your expensive climbing gear while someone else carries your oxygen and everything else you need to survive is not really proving anything, except perhaps that you have a lot of money.

Also, consider the fact that Sir Edmund Hillary did it over sixty years ago, wearing little more than a tidy wool sweatshirt and a parka. Not to mention the Sherpas who run up and down that thing several times a day wearing not much more than a beanie and underpants. If you're prepared to do that, then I say, have at it.

Otherwise, do your kids a favor and don't die unnecessarily for the sake of winning Instagram for a few weeks.

PREGNANCY

218
Maternity photo shoots are not compulsory

Pregnancy photos are becoming as overblown and portentous as wedding photos. All you need is one good shot every couple of months to document a pregnancy. It doesn't need to be a major production. Enough with the Demi Moore-style naked shots with the "hand bra" and the leg stepped forward to conceal the minge. No more wistful cradling of the tum-tum. And let's ban "heart hands" on bellies. I'm more than happy to see you photographed while pregnant, I just want to see something new. Oh and remember, you don't have to be naked. I can still see that you're pregnant when you have clothes on. (Having said that, hats off to Amy Schumer for running naked in UGG boots through Central Park for her pregnancy shoot. That was funny.)

219
You don't have to call it a "belly"

It can still be a stomach. For some reason everyone feels obliged to call it a "belly" when they're pregnant.

220
Pregnant women are not magic lamps—don't rub them

Always ask first. Or better yet, wait for the pregnant woman herself to suggest the idea—but don't be surprised, or annoyed, if she doesn't. Not everyone likes their tummy rubbed. (My dog can't believe I just said that.)

221
Keep pregnancy announcements simple

There's a growing trend for people to announce their second child by photographing their first child holding up the ultrasound of the new baby—which is really off-putting because it kind of looks like your toddler is pregnant.

222
Gender-reveal parties are not a thing

If you were thinking about having one of these, don't. Just have dinner with your friends and tell them you're having a boy or a girl. That's all anyone needs; in fact, I don't even need that, I'm happy to wait until the baby is born and have a look for myself.

SPECIAL SEALED SECTION
FOR MOMS

I am aware I am not a mother. However, I do have a mother, so I know what they're like. These rules are for mothers everywhere.

223
Calling something "delicious" does not make it so

Mothers have an odd habit of thinking they can trick children into eating something simply by referring to it as "delicious." My mom still does it today.

"Would you like a slice of this delicious spelt loaf?"

"No thanks, Mom, I'd like a slice of bread that tastes like bread but hey, you go right ahead and tuck into that 'delicious' loaf that tastes like grass and wet cement."

224
Don't fixate on irrelevant details

If your teenager is talking to you, you need to act casual—be interested but not too interested, just let them tell the story and take what you're given. Do not, however, frighten them off by peppering them with specific questions.

My mother, for example, always wanted to know about the numbers; she was obsessed with how many people were present at any party I went to. Yes, she was interested in knowing who was there, but mostly she wanted to know how many were there. I don't know why. I'm sure she thought I was being recalcitrant when I shrugged and said "I dunno" every time she asked but, the thing is, I genuinely did not know. I still don't. To this day, once the number of people goes above eight, I'm clueless. Could be ten, could be sixty-three, could be four score and seven. I have no idea. I am the opposite of Rainman. And whenever I watch Dustin Hoffman in that scene where the waitress drops the box of toothpicks and then Ray correctly identifies exactly how many are on the floor in a matter of seconds—"246, 246 toothpicks total, 246"—I think about my mom and how happy she would have been if only I'd had those kind of skills.

"How many people were at the party?"

"246, 246 people at the party, Mom, 246 total, 246."

225
Don't chase children with food

No one will die if they leave the house without breakfast. There's no need to pursue your child down the street waving a banana and trying to stuff it into their bag as they attempt to get away from you.

226
Keep a packet of fresh tissues at hand

Mothers are always being asked for tissues. Always. And yet for some reason, they can never produce a fresh one. Admittedly they can always produce a tissue, of sorts. Usually some screwed-up, lint-covered rag they've fished out of the bottom of their handbag, one that they insist is clean as they unball it and smooth it out while handing it to you. If you're a mom, you know that someone at some point during the day is going to need a tissue, so when you're grabbing your essentials—keys, purse, phone—why not grab a little packet of unused tissues and throw them in your bag too?

227
Don't use inappropriate analogies

Does your child really treat the place like a hotel? And if so, is that such a bad thing? Every hotel I've ever been to takes my credit card up front and I'm then held liable for all expenses. Maybe you should start treating the place like a hotel too, and charging them for everything from housekeeping to meals served in the hotel restaurant—or, as you probably call it, your kitchen.

Does their bedroom *really* look like a brothel? Have you ever walked in to find a fat sweaty man with his pants around his ankles and a bored-looking woman trying to act sexy while she digs around in a big bowl of condoms beside the bed? Or is the room just a bit messy? My guess is brothel workers keep their rooms quite tidy. I certainly don't imagine they have wet towels dumped all over the floor, piles of clothes on top of the bed, plus a dirty old bong and countless used cups and plates pushed under the bed; the bed is a workspace, after all—it's probably kept clear of all clutter. So let's not insult the sex workers by comparing them to your slovenly teenagers.

228
Stop wasting fruit

That's what you're doing every time you put an apple or an orange or a banana into a lunchbox. Save yourself some time and just put that thing straight in the trash—that's where it's going to end up eventually. The only uncertainty is whether it happens at school on the day or at home three weeks later when it's exhumed in a blackened and slimy state from the bottom of their school bag.

229
Don't ask your child if they will be warm enough

They don't know. They don't care. They don't have an answer. You're pissing into the wind with this one.

CHILDREN'S PARTIES

230
You don't have to invite the whole class

Seriously, it's okay to leave some kids out. Similarly, it's okay if your child is sometimes left out. We can't all be friends with everyone. It's unrealistic.

231
Don't waste money on gifts children won't appreciate

Chances are the first birthday a child will actually remember is their fourth birthday, so keep the money you would have spent on gifts for those first few birthdays and put it toward their education. I'm kidding, who cares about that? Take the money you would have spent on those first few birthdays and buy something nice for yourself instead. You deserve it. The kid will be just as happy with a roll of bubble wrap or a box of those foam packing peanuts. In fact, I know a three-year-old boy who desperately wanted a box of surgical gloves for his birthday. It cost his mom $3.99 and he has never been happier. Your kids will become an enormous and endless financial drain soon enough, so conserve money while you can.

232
No smash cakes

If you haven't heard of smash cakes, then please head to Facebook and post about how #blessed you are because I certainly wish I had never heard of them. A smash cake is exactly what it sounds like: a cake that parents with too much money buy for their child to "smash." Oftentimes they also hire a photographer to document this wanton destruction because who doesn't want a picture of a toddler covered head to toe in cake. Soooooooo cyute.

233
Drop the kids off and go

In days of yore (well, back in the '70s) my mother used to drop me at a classmate's birthday party by slowing the car down, shouting "tuck and roll," and then pushing me out the door. By the time I reached the house, she was out of sight and already enjoying her child-free afternoon.

Not so these days. Parents now tend to stick around at kids' parties. So not only do you have to entertain the kids, you have to entertain the parents too. Which is a lot of hard work. I realize there is a bit of a gray area when kids are still quite young. That's when you might actually want other parents to stay in order to help wrangle a house full of pre-Ks hopped up on sugar. But once those kids can competently toilet themselves and articulate things like: "Joshua has fallen off the trampoline and now his leg looks weird," lingering parents can be a real drag. To avoid any confusion, I suggest making it very clear on the invitation. Much like you would with a dress code. Simply state: "Please note, this is a Drop & Go event."

PETS

Putting rules for pets in the parenting section might seem offensive to some, but I gave it serious consideration and came to the conclusion that owning a pet and owning a toddler aren't really that different. There's a lot of cleaning up after them, a lot of stopping them from putting random objects in their mouths, a lot of rejecting other people's opinions on how to make them behave, and an awful lot of apologizing if they bite someone at day care.

234
Pick up your dog's poo

Once again, I start with the obvious. This is a genuine problem in dog parks where dogs are off the leash. You need to watch your dog like a hawk when he's off the leash, lest he run off and do a poo somewhere and you don't witness it. There's no philosophical debate about dog poo. It's not like when that tree falls in the forest and possibly makes no sound because no one is there to hear it. When a dog poos in the park, even if there's nobody around to see it, that poo still hits the ground, it still smells, and it still needs to be picked up, posthaste, by you, before someone steps in it.

235
Don't stand around talking at the dog park

Keep it moving people, keep it moving, circulate, walk those dogs. When people cluster, dogs cluster, and that's when fights start—between both the dogs and the people. Seriously, there is way too much spurious advice being doled out at the dog park by enthusiastic amateurs who have watched a few episodes of

The Dog Whisperer and now fancy themselves as professional dog trainers. Dog training is like parenting—unless someone asks you specifically for your opinion, best to keep it to yourself.

236
Never presume your animal is acting out of spite

Dogs don't chew your stuff or piss on the rug in order to get revenge. Spite is not in your dog's emotional repertoire. There is simply no such thing as a dog (or a cat) doing a "spite pee." If your pet is pissing on things or chewing things, he might be anxious or bored or agitated by something, but he's not being spiteful. Unless, of course, the animal is a hamster—those things are positively biblical in their quest for vengeance.

237
Dogs don't speak English

You have to teach a dog English, just like you would a toddler. You can't just get a puppy and say "sit sit sit sit sit" and expect him to know what that means. As for complex sentences, like "Baxter, be nice, be gentle, remember when you were a puppy, Baxter, you didn't like it when big dogs jumped on you, so be nice please!" Guess what? Baxter didn't get any of that.

238
If your dog does something wrong, apologize

It's mortifying when your dog does something wrong—whether he's aggressive toward another dog or jumps on a child or steals a sandwich out of a kid's sports bag or, in my dog's case, pisses on a lady in a fancy hat sitting in the park enjoying the sunshine. When these things happen, don't try to excuse or justify the behavior: "Oh I'm sorry, he really doesn't like black and white dogs," or "Sorry, he's a bit frightened of skateboards," or "Sorry, he really enjoys pissing on people in hats." Just apologize unreservedly—"I'm so sorry my dog pissed on you"—put your dog back on the leash and walk away.

239
Never say you hate cats if you haven't had a cat

How do you know? You can still say you prefer dogs, but don't say you hate cats. There is nothing hateable about a cat. And you'd know that if you'd ever had one.

240
There should never be more than one poo in a litter box

Your house does not have to stink just because you have a cat. I watch a lot of that show *My Cat from Hell* on the Animal Planet channel, and I see many people who claim that their cat goes outside the litter box. But when the cat-whisperer guy visits, you see the litter box is chock full of poo?! Well, no wonder the cat started crapping outside the box?! What cat wants to stand on top of a pile of poo in order to do another poo. Empty the litter box every time there's a poo in it. Every time.

FASHION

A Word about Fashion

It's a brave person who dispenses fashion advice. Fashion updates more often than my stupid phone's software, and my stupid phone's software needs updating all the time. (Which I really don't understand—why can't they get it right the first time?)

Over the years, I have committed many fashion errors and indeed a few crimes. The most serious of these occurred when I was just ten years old. I went out, in public, to a restaurant wearing gray corduroy knickerbockers paired with a matching gray flannel shirt that buttoned up on one side and had a high-neck ruffled collar—kind of House of Tudor meets frillneck lizard. The occasion was my tenth birthday and Mom had taken me shopping for a special birthday outfit to wear to my birthday dinner at The Black Stump—which, in my mind, was the fanciest restaurant in town. In reality it's the Australian version of Applebees. Was there anything more sophisticated than a chewy, well-done steak (I was young, I didn't know any better, that's how I requested it be cooked) and one of those delicious baked potatoes in foil that came accompanied by the famous Black Stump condiment caddy of sour cream, chives, and cubes of butter?

For some reason I decided the most appropriate way to dress for this sophisticated occasion was to dress like Prince— if Prince's favorite color had been gray and if he'd chosen to be a parking inspector rather than a fabulously purple music industry demigod.

I guess what I'm pointing out here is that I am possibly not the right person to be dispensing rules about fashion. But then again, one of my most important rules for life is: "Do as I say, not as I do."

$\longrightarrow$

GENERAL FASHION RULES

241
All buttons on or below the nipline must be done up

The simplest way to know whether a button should be done up or left undone is to draw an imaginary line across your chest from nipple to nipple—that's the "nipline"—any button that sits on or below that line should be done up. Important note for the ladies over thirty; put your bra on first, then draw the line.

242
Team jerseys are not for going out in

A woman wouldn't wear her softball kit to a nightclub, so men should apply the same standards and eschew the football jerseys and NBA uniforms when it comes to selecting clothes for a night out.

243
No shoe mash-ups

Ever since German physicist Albert Klochwireless successfully combined the clock and the radio in 1932, humans have been desperate to mash things together, largely without success. The mocha is one such example, combining two perfectly satisfactory stand-alone beverages into one unpleasant drink that doesn't taste quite right. Is it a coffee that tastes a bit like chocolate? Or is it a hot chocolate that tastes a bit like shit?

Some of the more recent mash-ups come courtesy of the shoe world. The particular shoe mongrel that comes to mind is the high-heeled sneaker. A completely pointless piece of footwear. What you have is a sneaker that is no longer comfortable—which, when you think about it, is the sneaker's greatest attribute. And a high heel that is no longer elegant—which is easily the high heel's *only* attribute.

The boot sandal is another strange shoe hybrid that keeps popping up—all the trappings of a boot but with the toe and the heel cut out, rendering it inappropriate footwear for both winter and summer.

244
Wear socks

Unless you're wearing sandals (or flip-flops) you should be wearing socks. It's really a question of hygiene. When I see a man wearing shoes with no socks, I don't think, *Ooh, that's a tidy ankle, what a treat to get a peek at that exposed joint!* I think, *Oh man, there is some serious fungus being harvested in those shoes.*

245
Keep your socks age-appropriate

Some people find the current "Happy Socks" trend offensive, especially when it's middle-aged men parading around in super-fun socks covered in cat faces and pineapples. Personally, I don't care what socks you wear, as long as you wear socks.

246
Forty-dollar rubber flip-flops are the same
as two-dollar rubber flip-flops

Spend your money elsewhere. Perhaps on a delicious sherry vinegar—which happens to be my favorite of all the vinegars.

247
No one looks good in Hammer pants

Hammer pants are so named because they originally came to our attention when they were worn by the rapper MC Hammer, who was what I like to call a gentleman rapper. He was around back in the day when rappers mostly referred to women as "ladies" or "fly girls" as opposed to the present day where we are all "bitches" and "hoes."

The distinguishing feature of the Hammer pant is the ridiculously low-slung, baggy crotch. They are large and billowy around the thigh area but they tighten around the calf and ankle. The more accurate name for these pants is "poo-catchers" because it really does look like you have mistaken your pants for a toilet. And after that description, you'd be forgiven for wondering why I have even brought them up. Surely Hammer pants are dead and gone, never to be seen again, except perhaps on *Yo! MTV Raps* late at night during a special early-nineties "Gentlemen of Rap" edition featuring Mr. Hammertime, Young MC, Tone Loc, et al.

But no. For some inexplicable reason, every ten years or so they rise again, appearing in fashion magazines, where they are worn by impossibly thin, beautiful models leaning against rocks by the sea or standing astride vintage bicycles. These waifs make the pants look not only super-comfy but somehow elegant too—fooling the rest of us into thinking, *Hmm, perhaps I do need some of those pants for next time I go to the coast and want to lean against rocks* ... Don't be fooled. When it comes to Hammer pants, remember the words of the very wise MC Hammer himself and don't touch them.

FASHION FOR THE OVER-FORTIES

248
Don't buy your entire wardrobe from REI

Or Eddie Bauer, Patagonia, or any of those other outdoorsy stores. Sure, the clothes are comfortable and they are very well serviced by a ridiculous number of pockets, but the truth is you're going out for fish and chips by the harbor, not trekking up to Base Camp 1.

249
Ladies, avoid anything too "fun" in the fashion department

Tops with appliqué or sequins are extremely difficult to pull off once you reach about forty. Young people get away with wearing them because it's ironic and kooky to dress like their crazy old aunt. Once you're forty, however, you just look like the crazy old aunt. But hang in there because . . .

250
Once you hit sixty, all bets are off

At sixty, suddenly you *are* the crazy old aunt and now is the time to break out the bedazzler and start styling up your denim jacket or your waistcoat or even an old wind jacket. Get creative with beads and glitter, get yourself a Michaels store account and, while you're at it, find some brightly colored tapered pants because you are officially a fun old bat. It's good times ahead as you see out your senior years in a riot of color and craft.

251
The older you get, the less denim you should wear

Between forty and forty-five is a good time to start thinking about alternatives to jeans. Especially if you're a man. You don't have to give them up completely just yet, but perhaps start phasing them out, because once you hit retirement age you need to give up wearing jeans altogether. Coincidentally there is a new Coen brothers film coming out about this exact rule, it's called *No Jeans for Old Men*.

252
If you look like a rolled roast, go up a size

I used to be a size 4, but I'm not anymore. However, after years of reaching for the same size, it's a hard habit to break. And there's no question, I'm in slight denial about my increase in girth, so a lot of the time I still try to pour myself into a size 4. Invariably it's way too tight, grips me in all the wrong places, and highlights every lump, bump, and fat roll. It really does look like I've been trussed around the midsection with butcher's twine. Time to go up a size and be comfortable.

DENIM AND LEATHER

253
Denim is for jeans and jackets

Not slacks or coats.

254
Only really hot people can wear double denim

Life is unfair sometimes.

255
Leather pants are best avoided

The window for wearing leather pants is even more elusive than the one where a pear becomes just ripe enough to eat but not so ripe that it becomes mushy. It's somewhere between the ages of nineteen and twenty-one—but even if you're the right age, that's still no guarantee you can pull off leather pants.

Leather pants are difficult to wear both literally and figuratively. They are physically very heavy and they don't have a lot of give, which makes them hard to get on and off. Once on, they don't breathe. At all. And forget about "wicking" properties. Any sweat you produce inside those leather pants is staying in there till you get them off and wipe them clean. On top of that, you have to be the perfect size. Long-haired ladies in leather pants who are too thin risk being mistaken for the lead singer of an eighties hair metal band. Yet anyone even slightly larger than a size zero risks being mistaken for a couch.

SPECIAL SEALED SECTION
TATTOOS

The following section has been sealed because it's for cleanskins only. There's no point in tattooed folk reading these rules, you've already gone and drawn on yourselves. I'm curious to see whether Generation Z and the current crop of youth will reject tattoos when they get older. In the world they inhabit, everyone from their spinster aunt to their grandad to their quirky geography teacher has tats, and surely that makes them predictable and conformist. Perhaps in the future, not getting a tattoo will be seen as a rebellious act.

256
No tattoos above your collarbone

If I have to explain why you shouldn't tattoo your neck and face, I can't help you. Put the book down and walk away.

257
Don't get a tattoo because you lost a bet

Far better to renege on the bet and take a bit of flak for a few days than be stuck with a stupid tattoo for the rest of your life. People will quickly forget that you lost a bet about who could eat the hottest curry (which is a really dumb bet anyway—why do men think eating spicy food is such an achievement?), but they won't forget that pointless tattoo of a red chile on your shoulder because that's going to be there forever. And "bet tattoos" are never high quality, so there's every chance your "chile" will look more like an angry pointy red penis with a bend in it. Sweet.

258
No tribe? No tattoo for you

If you choose to get "inked" with tribal tattoos, you must be able to prove your affiliation with said tribe plus give the full history of that tribe and the specific cultural significance of each of the tattoos you have selected.

259
No butterfly or dolphin tattoos

This is because as your body sags and spreads you'll soon find yourself sporting a dirty old moth in place of the butterfly, and where you once had a majestic dolphin leaping across your deltoid now there's a sad, lumpy creature that looks more like a dugong.

260
Decide on your tattoo, then wait a year

Then if you still believe it's a good idea, wait one more year. Better to be safe than sorry you got stuck with something you thought was cool in your twenties.

If I'd been tattooed back in the day, I might now be a middle-aged lady with a tramp stamp of the Bear surfboard logo from *Big Wednesday* across my lower back or a vague likeness of The Fonz from *Happy Days* besmirching my calf. And there's no doubt that The Fonz "portrait" would have been one of those heavily shaded "famous person" tattoos you see that makes you do a double take because at first glance, it looks like Marilyn Monroe (or Elvis or James Dean or whoever) was actually black?!

The "wait a year" rule is even more important if you are thinking about getting a written statement tattooed on yourself. Things like "blood is thicker than water," which sounds so profound after a few beers but in reality is just a scientific fact. It's like getting "sea water is undrinkable" or "it gets harder to lose weight as you get older" tattooed around your neck. Some things don't need to be said. Especially in permanent ink on your person.

261
Never have someone's face tattooed on your knee

It might seem like the perfect spot when you're younger—after all, it's round and face-shaped! But as you age, so too will the person you have immortalized on your knee and eventually they'll start to look like they are having a stroke.

262
Never have someone's knee tattooed on your face

To be fair, this is not something I've ever seen before, I just thought I'd try to get ahead of the curve and make a preemptive rule.

PIERCINGS AND OTHER HOLES

263
Maximum two piercings per head

Please choose wisely.

264
Don't make large holes in your ears

Ten years ago, no one would have believed we would ever need a rule to stop people from stretching their earlobes to the point where you can stick your fists through them. A special note to any kids thinking about getting these: it's not like piercing your ears. The gaping holes you've created will not simply close over and heal themselves, you will need surgery to repair them. So if you must pay tribute to the traditions of the Maasai, perhaps think about shaving your head or wearing a fetching red robe. They also drink a lot of milk-based beverages and wear beautiful beaded jewelry. I'm just saying there are plenty of less permanent ways to appropriate someone else's culture.

SUNGLASSES

265
Sunglasses are for outside

The clue is in the word: sunglasses are glasses that protect your eyes from the sun. So unless you are Corey Hart, you don't need to wear them at night, and unless you're Stevie Wonder, you don't need to wear them inside.

266
Don't stow your sunglasses on the back of your neck

Either take them off and put them away when you no longer need them, or pop them on top of your head. But never on the back of your neck. "Dudes" in Florida appear to be the main offenders when it comes to "backnecking" sunglasses in the United States but the backneck crime capital of the world, without a doubt, is the Gold Coast in Australia.

267
Sunglasses are not a wig

This is a special rule for bald men. Wearing sunglasses atop your head does not hide your hairlessness; we all still know you're bald.

MAKEUP

268
Ladies, go easy with the contouring

Contouring is something the Kardashians introduced to the mainstream; however, it is also something best left to professional makeup artists. Applied expertly, contouring can subtly change the appearance of your face by shading certain areas—it can draw attention away from a double chin or correct a bumpy nose or give you sharply defined cheekbones where once you had none.

Unfortunately, these days most contouring is being done with the heavy hand of an enthusiastic amateur, which is why we are seeing a lot of gals contouring themselves so excessively that they start to resemble an extra in the *Lion King* musical or Rum Tum Tugger from *Cats*.

269
Big false eyelashes look like big false eyelashes

You are fooling no one with those thick, heavy, fake, stick-on lashes. There's not a single person looking at you thinking, *Wow, that woman's eyelashes are amazing!* Rather, we are all thinking, *Jesus, how is she managing to keep her eyes open with those giant black tentacles glued to her lids?*

270
Less is more

This is an all-ages rule. When you are young, your skin is youthful and dewy, there's no need to put a thick coat of paint on it.

And when you are older, it's even more important to back off—especially around the eyes—lest you start looking like a crepe-y old drag queen or Lesley Joseph in *Birds of a Feather*.

Drag queens (and Lesley Joseph), you are the exceptions to this rule; obviously, you all can go nuts.

271
Leave your eyebrows alone

There is quite the trend at the moment for stenciled eyebrows. Where once, drawn-on eyebrows were the purview of old ladies whose eyebrows had fallen out over the years, now more and more young people are choosing to Frida Kahlo themselves with a pair of heavy, drawn-on eyebrows.

The obvious problem with this is that you need to decide in the morning on your mood for the day. Should you draw on a pair of angry eyebrows? Or maybe surprised eyebrows? Or perhaps you fancy that you'll be spending a large part of your day making wry comments that require you to have one eyebrow raised while the other stays put.

The best solution to this conundrum is to put the crayon down and leave your eyebrows alone.

272
Never trust a woman in a lab coat at the makeup counter

You see these ladies in department stores all the time but, remember, the white coat is a total misdirect—this woman is neither scientist nor makeup artist. She is simply a sales assistant who likes to "have fun with makeup" (and she probably stole that coat from the Pond's Institute). As such, she is not to be trusted. If you do get sucked in and decide to sit down and let her do your makeup, be prepared to walk around for the rest of the day resembling Nanki-Poo from *The Mikado*.

MODELS

273
Models don't get to say that they were ugly or unattractive at school

Sorry, but no one believes you. Nor do we think it's upsetting that you were apparently "bullied" by kids who called you "lanky" or "Giraffe." Neither of these things is particularly insulting. You can't undo the fact that you won the gene lottery, just go with it.

Oh, and we don't believe that you "pig out" on burgers and fries either. Because if you did, you'd look like the rest of us.

AT THE MOVIES

A Word about the Movies

Years ago I met an English comedian named Ian in the dressing room of the London Comedy Store. He was quite possibly the most stylish man I had ever encountered, certainly on the comedy scene, where comedians (straight ones, anyway) aren't exactly known for their sartorial elegance. Ian was a mod. He was tidy and unbelievably well dressed: he looked like he'd just stepped out of the pages of a 1969 magazine called Mod Style Gents *or* Fine AF Monthly. *What I remember most about Ian, however, was the fact that he hadn't been to the movies in twenty years.*

At first, when he told me that, I didn't believe him—I thought he was doing a bit but he wasn't. For a start, he wasn't that type of comic, he didn't do bits at you in dressing rooms (which was another reason to like him), but also he happened to be telling the truth. He said that he found it too tense to watch films in the company of complete strangers, whose behavior you had no control over.

He told me the last time he had gone to the movies, all those years ago, it had ended very badly. A fellow moviegoer sitting behind him wouldn't stop talking. Ian shushed him numerous times but the man would not be shushed. So Ian punched him. It's the sort of thing we all feel like doing but (fortunately) no one actually does it.

Being an otherwise reasonable man, Ian realized immediately that he couldn't just go around punching people because that is not how a civilized society works. However, he also realized that he couldn't not punch someone who kept talking during a movie. His rather extreme solution was to simply stop going to the movies. I adored his conviction. Twenty years! That's a long time.

Ian now lives with his wife and three children in the French countryside where he is easily the best-dressed farmer the world has ever seen. It's approaching forty years since he has been to the movie theater, and therefore I would like to dedicate the following section to him.

———————————————————→

FOR MOVIE-GOERS

274
No talking once the previews start

Low-volume talking through the ads is permitted but, once the previews start, stop talking. The previews should be seen as an extension of the movie and, of course, we all know there is no talking during the movie. I haven't written that as a rule because I think it's actually the law, and if it isn't, it should be—there should be cinema police who arrest people for talking during the movie.

275
Wait and let the story unfold

If you can't understand what's going on, chances are it will become apparent in time, just be patient. There's nothing worse than when a new character appears on-screen and someone says, "Who's that?" or "What's he doing?" Hey! No one knows yet, they just appeared, let the story unfold.

276
Support the lone shusher

If someone in the theater has the courage to shush the chatter, then be sure to add your endorsement with a loud "Yes! Shush!" or even a "Hear, hear!" I wouldn't normally advocate using "hear, hear" outside of the British Parliament in the 1600s, but it's dark in the theater, no one will see you. It's really important to back up the shusher; they are showing real courage and also performing an essential service. They're like the first responders of cinema.

277
Avoid noisy snacks and crinkly wrappers

If you must munch chips during a movie (and I wish you wouldn't), rip the bag open quickly. Don't do that thing where you laboriously pry it open, bit by bit. You're just prolonging the agony. Rip that band-aid off and get on with your infernal crunching.

I was told it would be an indication of mental illness to include a rule that said "Please suck your chips." So I won't. But I want you to know that I'm thinking it.

278
Turn your phone off

Please note the exact wording of this rule, which is turn your phone *off*. Recently movie theaters have lowered their standards and the pre-movie announcement now requests, very politely, that you turn your phone to silent. However, if it's only on silent, you'll be tempted to keep checking it throughout the film. And when you check your phone in the theater, the screen lights you up like a lone streetlamp on a dark country road and irritates anyone within a six-seat radius. So turn it off, sit back, and enjoy the film uninterrupted.

Nothing will happen in that ninety minutes that can't wait until you leave the movies. And if, god forbid, something life-shatteringly awful *does* happen, isn't it better that you got to enjoy that last ninety minutes completely worry-free, especially now that your life has taken a complete turn for the worse?

279
Leave a courtesy buffer seat

Unless the movie is completely sold out, never take the seat immediately next to someone else. Always leave at least one or two seats between you and the next punter.

I go to the movies by myself a fair bit (admittedly it's not always my choice, a lot of people refuse to go anywhere with me because of all my rules) and, when I do go alone, I like to have what I call a "seat moat" all around me. Imagine me in my seat, with three free seats in front of me, one empty seat on either side, and then three more empty ones behind me. A perfect ring of personal space all around. That's the dream.

280
Movie then dinner, never dinner then a movie

This is really just common sense. If you go to dinner first, you'll be clock-watching throughout your meal and potentially rushing your food in order to make it to the movie on time.

More importantly, however, seeing the movie first gives you something to talk about over dinner. Ideal for a first date, when you don't really know each other, but also perfect for a couple who has been together for a long time. Being able to discuss the movie saves you from looking like that couple who has run out of things to say to one another and whose sole job it is now to sit in restaurants and depress other couples who look across at you and think, *Shit, I hope we don't become that couple*, or *Shit, I wonder how long before we become that couple?*

SPECIAL SEALED SECTION
POPCORN

If you have read my previous book, you will already know that I have a lot of completely irrational and totally unenforceable rules about popcorn. I am very much aware that these rules make me seem like a real nutjob, which is why I have metaphorically sealed this particular section. Consider this an appendix for serious rule enthusiasts only.

281
Don't eat popcorn at the movies

If I had my way, popcorn would be banned from cinemas. I actually like popcorn, but I don't think it should be eaten in confined windowless spaces such as movie theaters. Commercially produced popcorn stinks far more than the popcorn you make for yourself at home. The artificial stench of over-heated oil and synthetic butter flavoring is nauseating and there's no escaping it at the movies. The noxious popcorn miasma hits you the minute you walk into the foyer and it gets even worse once you sit down in the actual theater—because the only thing more offensive than the smell of popcorn is the smell of masticated popcorn. And that's exactly what you get when a room full of people sit in the dark and chomp away on that stuff with their mouths open.

282
You don't need a trashcan-size bucket of popcorn

Just get a small one. The large ones are stupidly large. It's physically impossible to eat that much popcorn because your face can't cope with that amount of salt. Your mouth starts to pucker and it gets harder and harder to push each kernel through what has become a very restricted opening between your shrivelled-up lips. That's usually the time you put your enormous tub of popcorn under your seat, promptly forget about it, and then kick it over when you get up to leave. It then gets ground into the carpet and the popcorn-stink cycle is complete.

This rule is especially relevant for parents taking kids to the movies. A small popcorn is ample; there is nothing worse than seeing a kid with a box of popcorn bigger than their head. Sometimes they can't even see past the popcorn to watch the movie properly.

On top of all that, there's the outrageous cost. Popcorn costs about ten cents to make and yet movie theaters charge you half a week's wages for a box of it. When you add that to the price of a ticket, it's surprising that anyone can still afford to go to the movies at all. At the risk of sounding like a Mom's Handy Hint website, I suggest being more organized and buying all your popcorn and snacks at the supermarket before you get to the theater. It will not only save you money, but if everyone starts doing it movie theaters might eventually realize no one is buying their hot smelly popcorn and get rid of it.

283
The handful of popcorn must be smaller than your mouth

Don't take large fistfuls of popcorn and push and shove them into your mouth like a toddler forcing a square peg into a round hole. If popcorn is spilling back into the feed-bucket or onto your lap and the floor around you, then you're taking too much. I realize it's dark and no one can see, but that's no reason to suddenly start eating like a bulimic possum. Slow down, take smaller "handfuls," and chew. With your mouth closed, obviously.

284
Get an ice cream instead

My ideal movie snack is ice cream. Whether it's in a cone or a cup. The beauty is it doesn't make much noise and you've almost always finished by the time the movie starts anyway. And if you're at a good movie theater, you can also enjoy a nice glass of red wine. If the theater you're frequenting doesn't serve wine, or they serve it in plastic cups, find a better theater.

Quality theaters are easily identified. All you need to do is ask two simple questions:

1. *Do you serve wine in glass stemware?* The answer should be "yes, of course."
2. *Do you screen movies with Rob Schneider in them?* The answer should be "no, of course not."

FOR MOVIEMAKERS

This is a handy section for anyone writing or making a movie. If you think you have come up with something that seems a little unbelievable or not quite accurate, this quick checklist will help you.

285
Women wear shower caps when they shower

For a woman, washing and drying your hair can be a fairly time-consuming ordeal and not something you want to do every day. If a woman can get away without washing her hair, she will. Yet whenever women shower in the movies, they seem completely unconcerned about how long it is going to take to wash and dry their hair, and they almost always stick their entire head under the shower, wetting down a perfectly good blowdry that would easily have lasted another day or two.

286
Women wash themselves to get clean, not to get off

No woman runs her soapy hands all over herself in a languid, sensual way—she methodically scrubs her areas.

287
Women don't have pillow fights

Not even when they're at college and living in dorms with roommates. Certainly no woman has ever had a pillow fight in her underwear. Pillow fights only happen in male movie directors' minds.

288
No one has sex on the kitchen floor

Why would you? Sure, the sexy times might start in the kitchen but people always move it to the bedroom. Not the kitchen counter. The bedroom is just down the hall, it has a comfortable bed in it. No matter how urgent you are, you can always call a thirty-second time-out to move proceedings to the bedroom.

289
Food fights don't happen in civilized households

There is no mother in the world who would tolerate a food fight. And certainly none that would encourage one. That scene where a child playfully throws a piece of spaghetti across the table, gets a shocked look from "Mom" that soon spreads into a naughty, knowing smile from Mom as she reaches into her own plate of pasta and throws an even bigger handful of spaghetti across the table? You know that scene? Well, it's never happened.

290
Young children don't speak in snappy witty rejoinders

Not many adults do either. But pithy comebacks from kids and sage counsel from children wise beyond their years are particularly grating and unrealistic.

291
Don't let the actors spit

This is a rule for directors. Actors sometimes get so worked up and "in the moment" that a bit of spit comes out during their dialogue. I'm not sure whether Daniel Day Lewis actually invented spit-acting, but he certainly took it to a new level.

The other serial offender/camel is Al Pacino. He likes to shout, and he likes to spit, quite often all over his costars; and for an audience, that can be quite distracting.

Therefore, the rule for directors is, when there's too much spit flying around and especially when someone has a bit of spit yawing up and down in a string between their lips, please call cut and go again.

292
No hitting on younger women

This is a rule for both on-screen and off. One of the main issues the #MeToo movement brought to the fore was that of older men hitting on younger women, with the men taking advantage of the power dynamic and the fact that they were the more senior members of the production. Now, I don't think older women necessarily enjoy being hit on by old men either; however, at least they are more likely to have the confidence and experience and, most importantly, the seniority to tell the old men to fuck off.

And perhaps if movies stopped casting much younger women to play the love interests of older men, then men would stop thinking that going out with much younger women is the norm. Don't get me wrong, I think young women are awesome—youth is undeniably seductive in its physical beauty—but speaking as an older woman with a lot of older women friends, my god we're an interesting bunch. I actually don't understand why older men don't want to get involved with women their own age. Seriously, we're pretty great. But then I guess I don't understand the urge to wank into a plant either. So what do I know?

AT THE SHOPS

A Word about Sunday Shopping

There used to be a corner shop in every neighborhood that sold a bit of everything. Essential items like milk, bread, packets of French onion soup, and candy for one cent apiece. When I think now about how long kids used to spend in front of the candy counter directing the obliging shopkeeper to give them "one of those and two of those, one of the red things at the front . . . and um . . . how much are the snakes? Yep, okay, one more of those . . ." all to make up a treat bag worth the grand total of ten cents, it seems like shopkeepers back then were idiots—albeit incredibly patient and kind and generous idiots.

In our area, the corner shop was referred to as "The Robbers." As in "Hey, can someone pop down to The Robbers and get some milk?" So called because they charged ridiculously high prices, which they got away with because they stayed open late and they were open on Sundays. That used to be the holy grail, to find a shop that was open on Sunday—it was the near-impossible dream. But now that dream has come true and it's come true in spades. What shop isn't open on Sunday? Shopping centers are the new church; these days when Sunday rolls around, the whole family heads off to worship at the mall.

I realize it's extremely convenient to be able to do your shopping on a Sunday, but I sometimes wonder whether it's a particularly fun way for children to spend the weekend—being dragged around a shopping center to purchase some much-needed homewares, like an oversized vase full of sticks or some forty million thread count sheets or a milkshake maker (you need a special maker for milkshakes now—apparently blenders don't make milkshakes anymore).

But then again, it could be worse. I'd take standing around in Kmart while my mom decided if she needed a chocolate fountain any day over sitting in a pew listening to a priest drone on about a two thousand-year-old street hustler who turned water into wine.

SHOP ASSISTANTS

293
Don't call anyone older than you "darling"

Or "darlin" or "babes" or "sweetie" or "hun," or any other bizarrely affectionate and over-familiar term of endearment. There is nothing more off-putting than walking into a shop and having a fresh-faced twenty-something greet you with, "Can I help you, hun?"

By the way, this rule is moot for anyone from the American South. Down there, referring to someone as "hun" or "darlin" is standard. They're born doing it and they couldn't stop doing it if they tried. It's in their DNA and it's neither sexist nor patronizing, it crosses all ages and genders—everyone is called "hun" or "darlin." Point is, it's charming coming from Tammy in Texas, but not so much from Sloane in Santa Monica.

294
Keep your banter vague

For some reason, everyone working in retail these days is desperate to know how your day is progressing. It's such a specific question: "How's your day been so far?" I'm afraid I don't have an answer to that question, especially at 9:30 in the morning when the day has barely begun. If you happen to be dealing with someone who genuinely wants to tell you how their day has been (like my friend Liz) then, trust me, they will volunteer that information without any prompting. She loves to give the sales assistant her life story, but she is a rare exception. With everyone else, you should just assume they are having an okay day—in fact, it was probably a pretty good day right up until you ruined it with your dumb question.

And further to this rule, never ever ask anyone over forty: "Got any plans for the weekend?" We don't. The clue is in the item on the counter in front of you. I'm buying big white granny-pants and a comfortable beige bra, not the sort of thing worn by someone who goes clubbing, or attends music festivals, or does anything else of interest on the weekend.

295
Acknowledge the customer standing at the counter

I will happily wait for you to finish whatever it is you are doing or pretending to do as long as you look up at me and say, "I'll be with you in a minute." And you don't even have to say it with your mouth, you can say it with your eyebrows and a small nod. On the whole, most people, even some New Yorkers, will wait patiently, provided they are acknowledged.

296
No hiding when you are supposed to be manning the register

I don't know where the register staff at Macy's disappear to every time I need to pay for something, but it's uncanny the way not a single person can be found at any register in any department once I am ready to make my purchase.

There have been several occasions when I have been forced to stand near the exit waving a prospective purchase through the sensors, setting off the alarms and shouting, "I am going to steal this Dutch oven if no one comes to serve me!"

297
Accept payment for goods at any and all registers

A good salesperson will find a way to take your money at whatever register you approach. It might mean opening a register specially for you or it might mean escorting you to the correct department and then jumping in behind that register. Either way, a decent sales assistant should just tappety-tap their staff number into the register and take your money. Because that's the job.

Some of the younger staff, however, tend to get rather separatist and refuse to allow cross-pollination of departments, especially if it means doing some work. After all, it's much easier to pass a customer off and send them elsewhere. For example, I once had a young woman refuse to let me pay for a wooden spoon in the underwear section. She said I had to take it back to kitchenware and pay for it there. I wish I'd had the presence of mind to insist that the spoon *was* from the underwear department and that I'd found it in a bin marked "special sex-spanking tools." Just to see the look on her face.

ATTENTION, SUPERMARKET SHOPPERS

298
Don't get aggressive with the plastic shopping-demarcation divider

Some people get really testy when you start placing your items on the belt too close to theirs, and they will pick up that plastic divider thing and make a point of using it not only to mark the separation but also to push your items back a bit. There's really no need to panic, no one is trying to trick you into paying for their items, nor does anyone want to steal your dumb tater tots.

299
Once at the checkout, you are only allowed to run back for one item

If you've forgotten any more than one item, surrender your place in the line and go and finish your shopping properly.

300
Don't be sucked in by this week's "special buy" at Aldi

You don't need a log splitter, even at that unbeatable price.

301
Don't collect plastic trash at the checkout

Supermarkets call these things "collectibles" but what they really mean is "useless bits of shit." I can guarantee your limited edition set of miniature plastic groceries will never appear on a future episode of *Antiques Roadshow*.

BIG SUPERMARKETS

302
Don't try to trick customers into buying your store brands

If your cheese is any good, I'll buy it. But don't insult my intelligence by packaging your own brand cheese to look like Murray's Cavemaster Reserve and then moving the Murray's Cavemaster Reserve right up high, out of my eyeline (and reach). You think I won't notice and will just buy your cheese instead without realizing, but I won't. Because I'm quite stubborn. And I have eyes. I'll either climb up the shelves and get the Murray's Cavemaster Reserve myself, or I'll wait for someone tall to come along and ask them to get it for me. What I won't do is be tricked into buying your generic store-brand cheese.

303
Program your self-service checkouts to expect the obvious

For example, placing a bag in the bagging area should not be unexpected; it's the bagging area, it's for bags.

304
Don't complain about shoppers making mistakes

If you want to make sure avocados don't get scanned "accidentally" as potatoes, go back to paying real people with eyes to work at your checkouts.

SPECIAL SEALED SECTION
FITTING ROOMS

I have sealed this section because I assume it's of interest to ladies only. I know there are some men who are interested in fitting rooms, but it's a very different kind of interest, one that I really can't get my head around. You read about these men every now and again in salacious news stories—they are the perverts who put hidden cameras in women's fitting rooms. And I have no idea why they do it, because I have rarely seen anything good looking back at me from the mirror in the women's fitting room.

Once, while attempting to squeeze into a too-tight swimsuit, I toppled over and headbutted the wall. The loud bang obviously alarmed the sales assistant, who immediately pulled back the curtain and asked, "Is everything okay in there, sweetie?" Clearly everything was not okay, especially not now that I was on display to the entire shop. Everyone could see me leaning with my head "resting" against the wall, unable to right myself due to the swimsuit trapped tightly around my thighs. Fortunately, I am a stickler for the rule of keeping one's underpants on while trying on swimsuits, so at least I wasn't busted with my bush out. However, that was of little consolation as I tried to fend off the young woman who had started to manhandle me in a bid to stand me upright. She then unnecessarily offered to

bring me a larger size. I say "unnecessarily" because I had no
plans to stick around; as soon as my pants were back on, I was
hightailing it out of there. Hopefully that young sales assistant
will purchase a copy of this book and make a note of the most
important fitting room rule:

305
No one but the person getting changed is allowed to touch the curtain

This rule pertains mostly to sales assistants but also to mothers
who love to whisk that curtain back without warning so as to
expose the vulnerable half-naked changer within. These types
of people also have a warped sense of time; for them thirty
seconds feels like an eternity, which is why, less than a minute
after you've entered the fitting room, they are simultaneously
asking, "How's it going in there?" and palming back the curtain.

306
The curtain must be bigger than the gap it is covering

It's unbelievable that this still needs to be said. It feels like women
have been complaining about fitting room curtains that don't go
far enough across ever since fitting rooms and curtains were
invented. It's a very simple formula: you measure the gap, then
order a curtain that is one and a half times that gap.

I've often wondered whether it was a women's clothing shop
owner who was responsible for ordering the rock they rolled in
front of Jesus's tomb. That would explain how the tomb came
to be empty three days later. JC obviously just slipped out the
huge gap left on one side.

307
No mirror, no sale

I imagine it was a man who came up with the idea of not putting a mirror in the fitting room. The thinking behind this master stroke of psychology is that if a woman is forced to come back out into the shop in order to see herself in the mirror, the sales assistant can leap into action and start telling her how amayyyyzing she looks, thus increasing the likelihood of a sale.

There are two major flaws in this strategy. Firstly, it vastly underestimates a woman's intelligence. I'm not an idiot, I know when I look like a potato wearing a cardigan and no fast-talking sales assistant is going to convince me otherwise. Secondly, it fails to take into account the fact that there won't be any interaction with any salesperson—because the minute I discover there are no mirrors in the fitting rooms, I'm turning around and walking straight out of the shop.

308
You're in a fitting room, not an episode of *Cheers*

Everybody does not need to know your name. I am prepared to name and shame the store in question (it's Lululemon) because god knows they name and shame me every time I go in there. What is with all the questions, Lulu? Seriously, Lemon, why must you write my name on the fitting room door like I've been put in detention?

Also, I don't have an answer when one of your fit young things who works there starts quizzing me about what sort of exercise I do. Because I'm not looking for hot yoga pants or cold yoga pants or even tepid yoga pants. I don't need a "tank" for Pilates or a bra top for jogging in. I'm just after some pants to wear when I walk my dogs and occasionally remember to tense my glute muscles for a few steps. Or, let's be completely honest, to sit around and watch television in while thinking about all the exercise I'm going to do . . . starting tomorrow.

309
No men within a ten-foot radius of the fitting rooms

Some women like to take their husband or boyfriend clothes shopping with them, which I find odd. I don't want to shop with any man I'm dating because I don't want to have explain why the white shirt I'm buying is different from the half a dozen other white shirts I already own. I want to buy what I like and not feel guilty about it.

But my main issue with it is that clothes shopping never looks fun for the man. He looks more like a hostage than a willing participant as he sits bored out of his scone in that chair that shops place outside the fitting rooms. The BHC, I call it: the bored husband chair. And in a confluence of unfortunate factors, the shops that have the BHC also seem to have the DCG, the dreaded curtain gap. Now I'm not saying that someone else's bored husband would *want* to peer through that gap and look at me, I'm just saying he shouldn't have to. He's already suffering from extreme tedium, let's not punish him further with glimpses of things he will never be able to unsee. Do everyone a favor, ladies, and leave the partners at home.

TECHNOLOGY

A Word about Our Own Importance

At some point in recent history, we all became really important, apparently, which is why we believe we must be contactable at all times. Where once you would leave the house and, by extension, the phone, because it was attached to the wall, now we take the phone everywhere, including places we don't really need it, like the movies, the gym, the park, the bathroom, etc. All places where we are already engaged in an activity and shouldn't want to be interrupted.

I understand it's not just about being contactable. We rely on our phones for directions and also to make us look busy and important when we are alone in a cafe. I accept that the world has changed and that people aren't going to leave their phones at home. So my first rule for cell phones is a compromise. I'm letting you have your phone, I'm just not letting you eat it too . . .

MOBILE PHONES

310
Don't answer your phone if you're busy

You are allowed to ignore your ringing phone. You don't have to drop everything to answer it. You can let the call go to voicemail or simply make a note to call someone back later when you're not otherwise occupied. Remember, you're not obliged to prioritize the person on the other end of the phone who, for all intents and purposes, has just rudely interrupted you by screaming, "Pay attention to me!"

311
Use your inside voice

It's always preferable not to take a call if you are somewhere public, like on a bus or in a cafe or walking down the street. However, if you *must* take the call, use your inside voice and then turn it down even further. So let's say your outside voice is a ten; your inside voice should be a six and your mobile phone voice should be a four or a three. A lot of people get this rule ass-backwards and think their mobile phone voice should be an eleven. These people are ruining the world for everyone.

312
Don't walk and text

Pull over. Don't keep walking, and definitely don't stop dead in the flow of foot traffic and cause a Keystone Cop pileup behind you. Stop and step to one side to do your texting.

313
No using speaker-phone in public. Ever

Even worse than having to listen to someone talk on their mobile phone is being forced to endure *both* sides of the banal conversation because they are having it on speaker-phone. More than being rude and inconsiderate, it is exceptionally arrogant to assume that your conversation is interesting enough to broadcast.

As for the youths who like to subject us all to their "killer jams" on public transportation, it's a simple fact that your music would sound better through headphones. Honestly, I know nothing about speakers or woofers or subtweeters, but even I can hear that the tinny speaker on your iPhone is making your crappy taste in music sound even crappier.

314
Turn off the clackety texting noise

Texting should be a silent endeavor. No one should even know you're doing it. Young people, do us all a favor: take your parents' phones and turn off that infernal clacking sound for them.

315
Don't show anyone anything on a shattered screen

No one wants to look at a photo through a sad, fractured screen. You lose all showing privileges until you get that thing fixed.

316
No unauthorized swiping through someone's photos

When someone hands you their phone to look at a photo, you are supposed to look at the specific photo that is on the screen, comment appropriately, then hand the phone back. Don't take it upon yourself to browse through the rest of their photo library, swiping away left and right like you're on Tinder all of a sudden. You don't know what's on there—they could have all sorts of pics they don't want you to see. A note to my own friends and family: if you get to those photos of me and my cat in matching bonnets, you've definitely swiped too far.

317
Don't check your phone while someone is talking to you

Even if that person is really dull, it's extremely rude to pull out your phone and look at it while they are talking to you. Whether it's during dinner, while you're having a drink, or just chatting in the hallway at the office. Checking your phone is the equivalent of looking at your watch, yawning, and walking off to talk to someone else mid-conversation. Don't do it.

318
Put your phone away when a friend is driving

Your friend is not your Uber driver or personal chauffeur. In giving you a lift, they are doing you a favor. Were they to use their phone during the ride, you'd probably end up wrapped around a telegraph pole, so extend them the same courtesy and stay off your phone while riding shotgun.

319
Don't be a phone evangelist

Whether you choose Apple or Samsung or that brand the Chinese government can monitor (apparently), it's still just a phone. There's no need to proselytize about it in a bid to convert others. While it's entirely possible your phone is marginally better than the one your friend is using, the reality is no one is going to switch brands. So stop doing unpaid work for the phone companies. It's sad.

320
Never forget your mobile phone *is* mobile

This is a rule for people who like to take or make phone calls in the living room while others are present, usually watching TV. By all means, take or make your call, but do everyone a favor and move into another room to do it.

321
It's a phone, not a walkie-talkie

Don't be one of those people who holds the phone in front of their mouth and talks into it—just put it up to your ear. They've done the research, the results are in: holding it up to your ear and talking into it like a normal person won't kill you.

322
Don't leave a voicemail if it's important

This is actually just a private note for my friends and family. I never listen to my voicemails—if you need me to call you, just send a text.

EMAIL

323
Don't have an email address with more than one underscore

No one's writing that down. So unless it's the dummy email address you invented for giving to shop assistants (see next rule), pick a different permutation.

324
Invent a dummy email address exclusively for shop assistants

We all have enough garbage clogging our inboxes without being put on mailing lists by every shop we've ever spent a dollar in. So do what I do and just rattle off a pretend Gmail account whenever a person behind a cash register asks for your details. And if there actually happens to be someone out there with the email address kittyunderscoreflanflanunderscore123@gmail. com, I sincerely apologize for all the retail junk mail you must be receiving courtesy of my excessive shopping habits.

325
Don't fire off emails that just simply say, "Hey! Tell me all your news!"

Or any version of the above, such as *What's happening with you?!* or *Update me on your life!* That places the entire burden on the receiver to satisfy your random pang of neediness. It's up to you to contribute, to offer something of yourself that will in turn elicit a newsy response.

SOCIAL MEDIA

326
Don't use social media to communicate with your partner

Declaring feelings for your partner on social media has become quite the trend, even though it makes no sense whatsoever. Presumably, if they're your partner, you have their phone number, and there's a good chance you might even be living together—so next time you're overcome with feelings of love for them, why not send a quick text or, better yet, wait until they get home and tell them in person. Sending messages to a partner via social media is less about telling *them* something and more about telling the world how amazing *you* are. Look how nice you are sending appreciative, loving messages to your significant other. It's also a form of bragging, all that *so lucky to have this beautiful guy in my life, feeling pretty blessed right now hashtag sweetlove* is a not-so-subtle way of rubbing your happiness in everyone's faces. If you're really feeling so blessed, I suggest you call that beautiful guy direct 'cause I reckon he's a lot more interested in hearing about it than the rest of us.

327
Enjoy the event in real time, not via Facebook posts

You're fooling no one with those good-time party pics because if you were genuinely having a good time at the party, you'd be too busy having a good time at the party to be posting about having a good time at the party on Facebook.

328
Don't post pictures of yourself doing yoga

There is nothing more at odds with the philosophy of yoga than the world of Instagram. Yoga is supposed to be about self-reflection and inner peace and all that spiritual jazz. But how reflective and "in the moment" can you really be when you're standing on a rock at sunset in your best Lululemons while your friend snaps shot after shot of you warrior-posing it up with the waves crashing all around as you shout, "Oh my god, hurry up, Felicia, we're losing the sun!"

Again, I would implore you to be original. If you must post pics of yourself exercising, why not entertain me with a quick little TikTok vid of you grapevining it up, Richard Simmons-style.

329
Nobody wants to sign your change.org petition

I'm not disparaging your good intentions, I'm just suggesting there might be something more proactive you could do for a worthy cause that is clearly very close to your heart. Something that takes a little more effort than pressing the "send to all my contacts" button.

330
Don't make a celebrity death all about you

When a celebrity dies, social media turns into the morbidity Olympics. Public mourning quickly becomes a competitive arms race to determine who is the saddest of them all. It's already a blow that the celebrity is dead but what's really depressing is that they aren't around to defend themselves and tell the world they weren't actually friends with @mattnobody on Twitter or Instagram.

331
A brag is a brag is a brag

The term "humblebrag" was coined by Harris Wittels to call out the sort of faux humility people employ when they want to brag about themselves. For example, *I went out looking like a fat sweaty pig today and this cute guy still hit on me? How weird is that?* The only thing weird about it is that you just posted something that essentially says, *Holy shit, I am sooooo good-looking!* Another example of a humblebrag is when a comedian or musician or actor posts something like: *How embarrassing, sitting in a cafe right now and there's a giant poster with my face on it in the window!* If it's that humiliating, you could always leave the cafe or not sit down there in the first place, rather than tweet about it and draw everyone's attention to it.

Unfortunately, the word has now moved into the vernacular and people seem to think that by heading up their braggy post with the word "humblebrag," it makes it okay. It doesn't. It's merely an admission that you know you're being a faux-humble narcissist. If you must brag, own it. Head your post with *Blatant brag about me*—we'll all respect you more.

332
Don't resort to hack expressions

Things like: *Love you to the moon and back, Feeling blessed, Hashtag gratitude.* We've all heard them a squizillion times. Make an effort, say something new that you thought of yourself like: "Love you more than my dishwasher and washing machine combined!"

333
Use the term "going viral" correctly

It means something has millions of views and has spread across newsfeeds exponentially in the manner of a virus. A lot of people tend to say, "Oh my god, my post has gone viral!" when all their friends have liked something. But unless you're a Kardashian, it's doubtful you have enough friends to make your post go viral.

334
Dial down the "please share" neediness

I like to make up my own mind about whether to share something or not, and I do that based on whether it is share-worthy, not because someone has implored me to "please share this post!!" It's the same with reviews or podcasts that end by begging their listeners to "please leave us a five star review." If your podcast is any good I'll tell people about it, with my big mouth.

BLOGGING

Bloggers love to write "from the heart" but sometimes they write from their ass by mistake. And unfortunately there is no curator of the internet; it's not like a newspaper or a magazine where there's an editor in charge of what gets published. Anything goes in Blogtown—it's like the Wild West, there are no rules, and that's never a good thing. So think of me as the benevolent sheriff riding into town with all of my blogging rules to help make the World Wide Web a better place.

335
Don't presume people have hours to read your blog

Try to be concise. Much as you might like to write a stream of consciousness, people don't want to read it. Save your rambling innermost thoughts for your private diaries. When writing for public consumption, get to the point. Less waffle, more content. Limit your word count and think of it as writing an article instead of laying a blog.

336
Blogging won't make you rich

It just won't. No matter what people tell you about advertisers and people buying space on your hugely successful blog, it won't happen. So blog if you must, but do it because you enjoy it, not because you think you're going to make monster coin.

337
No topic, no blog

I realize this is difficult—believe me, I understand how hard it is to come up with a topic. In fact, I would go so far as to say that the hardest part of creating any content is coming up with the topic. I spent five years doing a segment on *The Project* every Tuesday and then another four years doing something similar on *The Weekly*. That's nine years of "bits." And for those nine years, the most torturous part of my week was not writing the jokes or filming the segment or remembering my lines in front of a live audience, it was coming up with the topic. But without a topic, you have nothing. Literally. However, many bloggers ignore this essential first step and just blog away. The thinking seems to be that if they admit they don't have a topic, then that absolves them, which is why you see a lot of blogs that start like this: *Hi guys, feeling pretty exhausted today, not really in the mood to blog but I know everyone's expecting a post from me so here goes . . .*

What usually follows is a meandering account of the blogger's day or week detailing why they feel bloated or tired (because they accidentally ate a pizza crust that wasn't gluten-free) or something about their painful hemorrhoids that are making it hard to sit down which is why they are standing up to write their blog today. In short, nothing anyone needs to hear about.

Remember, if you don't have a topic, don't blog. Make every post count.

338
Give me the recipe, not the story of your life

Recipe bloggers are notorious for using the recipe to lure you into reading about their lives. I have rarely clicked on a link to a recipe and been lucky enough to have that recipe magically appear on the page before me. Instead, what usually happens is that I am forced to scroll through pages of irrelevant information about how the blogger was feeling on the day they first made this recipe or how their kids and hubby "love love love this dish!" There might be some arbitrary memories of their grandmother, who always loved this time of year and would sweep the autumn leaves into giant piles for the children to kick about in. Oh the hours of fun to be had in Gram-gram's yard. Yeah, yeah, whatever, blogger, just give me the old lady's recipe for chocolate chip cookies.

339
Limit of one blog per person

If you must start a new blog, delete the old one. Blogs are like internet landfill—we are rapidly running out of room on the World Wide Web, so please dispose of your old blog thoughtfully before starting a new one.

INSTRUCTIONAL YOUTUBE VIDEOS

340
Get to the point. Quickly

When making an instructional YouTube video, you want to think of it as court testimony and present the facts, just the facts.

Because when someone is seeking information on something—whether it be how to re-grout a shower recess, or crochet a bobble stitch, or use Excel to make a spreadsheet—everyone wants the same thing: simple, clear, step-by-step instructions. And that's it. No one is interested in tinkly music and fun graphics, and trust me when I say that absolutely no one wants to sit through a two-minute introduction where the "Tuber" waves hello and tells the viewer all about themselves and then explains what the video is going to be about.

These "filmmakers" have no idea how boring their presentations are because they don't have the benefit of a live audience. They just make the video, upload it, and that's it. They don't get to see the reaction of the viewer watching the video. So, for the YouTuber's edification and in a bid to improve the standard of YouTube clips across the board, I have transcribed a video I tried to watch recently and inserted the viewer's thoughts throughout.

YOUTUBER: "Hi, I'm Carly, I'm a stay-at-home mom and I lerve doing a bit of DIY around the house . . ."

VIEWER: *Good for you, Carly, not at all relevant, please move on.*

YOUTUBER: "Today I'm going to show you how to re-grout your shower recess."

VIEWER: *Yep, I know that already 'cause I googled "how to re-grout your shower recess" so get on with it.*

YOUTUBER: "Regrouting your shower is an easy way to give your bathroom a complete lift."

VIEWER: *Oh my god, I know! That's why I want to do it, come on already.*

YOUTUBER: "When I moved into this apartment the shower recess looked like this . . . not great, huh?"

VIEWER: *Don't care, your voice is annoying and I hate your hairdo, I'm starting to see why people leave abusive comments on YouTube, this is really irritating.*

YOUTUBER: "But now, thanks to a bit of hard work from me and my boyfriend, it looks like this . . ."

VIEWER: *Okay, forget it, I'm done. We're 49 seconds in, there's been no useful information, I'm clicking elsewhere. I came for instructions on grouting, Carly, not to be your gal pal. Also, how in god's name do you have a boyfriend when you are this boring? And no, I'm not going to leave you a five star review, I have a rule about that sort of thing.*

INTERNET COMMENTING

341
Don't read the comments section

You'll only work yourself into a bate, and possibly even be tempted to break the following rule.

342
Don't write in the comments section

It's like shouting into the air. Pointless and a sign of madness.

343
If you *must* write in the comments section, leave your full name

If you're not prepared to leave your full name and own your opinion, you don't get to share your opinion.

344
If you must write in the comments section *about me*, leave your full name *and* phone number

Because I would like to talk to you personally, mostly about your spelling and grammar. Helpful little things, like:

- YOU'RE is a contraction of "you are," as in "you are an idiot."
- YOUR is a possessive pronoun, as in "if you can't spell, that's <u>your</u> problem."

We may also need to discuss the difference between "bought" and "brought." And that you lend money *to* someone and you borrow money *from* someone but you never lend money *off* someone. Oh, and it's a moot point not a mute one . . .

345
If the humor article is not making you laugh, stop reading it

Comedy is subjective and we all find different things funny. Some people don't find anything funny. The good news is, there is actually a fair bit of content on the internet, so if you're not enjoying something, you can click on something else. No need to punish yourself by reading the whole thing, working yourself into an apoplectic state, and then shouting all over the comments section: "THIS ARTICLE IS NOT FUNNY!!" or "WHAT A STUPID WASTE OF TIME THIS ARTICLE IS!"

Shhhh, it's okay, close the article and either go watch a cat video, or maybe take some crack to calm down.

346
Fact trumps opinion

When presented with facts based on proven, peer-reviewed science, the phrase "Well, that's just your opinion" is not a valid argument. It's like being told: "According to the Bureau of Meteorology, yesterday it was 27 degrees outside," and you saying, "Well, that's just your opinion." No, no, that's a fact.

347
You must read the whole article before commenting

You cannot just look at the headline or the photograph attached to the article, draw your own spurious conclusions, and then spew out a comment. You are required to read the entire piece and make sure you understand not only the context but also the fact that the headline or photo may well have been ironic. Then you can comment. If you must.

348
Make your comment relevant to the post

Some people like to use the comments box to tell stories about themselves. They lure you in with one quick remark about the post and then segue very unsubtly into a story about their life. For example:

> *Hey, great article about brownies. I am currently in talks with a publisher about my memoir. It's about my childhood in Ireland. I was beaten by nuns, shared one pair of shoes with my three sisters, and my mother never made us brownies. Sadly, she was always too busy working. We discovered, years later, she was the village prostitute, we always thought she just had lots of boyfriends. Because she worked from home, we got sent to the library a lot. And that's how I fell in love with books. Books were my escape and now it looks like I will get one published. Yay! Thanks for posting.*

349
Don't engage with comment terrorists

These are people who like to hijack the comments and steer them off into uncharted and completely irrelevant territory. Essentially they are looking to provoke a fight with a stranger. For example, in a news item about a missing woman, the hijacker will seize control of the comments box by writing something like:

> *She looks like a botox whore!*

To which someone else will reply:

> *Shutup I know her, shes my friend and she so isn't a botox whore, why don't you go back to where you came from.*

And then the hijacker is straight back in with:

I'm from here u dumb slut, I guess U must be a botox whore to.

As you can see, it's now just a good, solid debate about a missing woman who may or may not have had Botox and who some people think might be a sex worker, even though the news item never mentioned either of those things. Don't let the comment terrorists win.

SPORTS

A Word about Sports

Contrary to popular opinion, I am not a sports-hater, nor am I completely ignorant about sports. In fact, back in the '80s I was quite the cricket fan. (And yes, we do call cricket a sport in Australia.) Everyone loved cricket back then and it was all thanks to the West Indies cricket team. In the '80s, most cricketers didn't look like athletes, they looked like beer-drinking, hotdog-munching, pot-bellied dads with terrible pornstar moustaches. Then along came the West Indies. The coolest, most athletic cricketers the world had ever seen. To put it into context for North American readers, their captain, Viv Richards, was like the Michael Jordan of cricket. Only cooler. Seriously, he was such a cool cat that none of us even noticed he had a lady's name, Vivian. Ask yourself, would Michael Jordan have been such an icon if his name had been Laverne? Yeah, all right, he probably would have. I mean, Air Lavernes, who doesn't want a pair of those sweet kicks?

Anyway, what I remember most about going to cricket games during that era was that there was no booing. People may have booed a display of bad sportsmanship, someone throwing a bat or a tantrum, but there was no booing the rival team for playing well and winning. You didn't boo because your team was losing, and you certainly didn't heckle and harass individual players from the stands.

Booing seems to have become accepted behavior these days, with fans very quick to get all Joaquin Phoenix-y from *Gladiator*, jeering and thumbs-downing the players they don't like. If I wanted to be trite, I'd say something like "and I think that really sums up everything that's wrong with the world today." But let's not be clichéd and platitudinous about things; after all, I'm not a sportsperson giving a post-game interview.

For this section, I wanted to be fair and impartial and acknowledge that society is made up of two different types of people, those who are really into sports and those who aren't. Thus I have provided rules for both sides.

$\longrightarrow$

FOR SPORTS FANS

350
No booing

Save your booing for when unpopular politicians turn up to watch a Broadway show (oh come on, I'm kidding!). My point is, you don't boo elite athletes for doing their job well.

351
You have Friday and Monday to talk about the weekend's game

That's it. One day of pre-game chatter and one day of post-game chatter, then let it go.

352
Keep your obscure stats to yourself

You might be the Rainman of football and know everything there is to know about every game ever played, but when you dominate the space with that kind of forensic knowledge, you completely alienate the lesser sports fans who are trying to join in. The way to bring a cross-section of people into the conversation is to casually drop a tidbit of salacious sports-related gossip. Everyone can get on board talking about the quarterback's wife who got busted for shoplifting or the player who tested positive for cocaine and Optifast shakes. No one, however, knows who you're talking about when you reference some legendary "four bagger" from a minor league baseball game back in 1928, even if it was "a classic."

353
No mocking the person coming last in the office bracket competition

Just appreciate that Jenny from Accounting is joining in.

354
Don't take a loss so seriously that it affects your mood for the rest of the day/week/month

Remember, it's just a game, nobody died.

FOR NON-ENTHUSIASTS

355
Never tell a fan: "It's just a game, nobody died"

Let someone be sad if their team loses.

356
Don't reject the entire notion of sports out of hand

There is nothing to be gained from loudly lamenting the fact that sports get more funding than theater. Sports are massively popular for a reason and that's because they're actually quite accessible. If you give it ten minutes, you can usually work out the rules for most games, which is more than can be said for Shakespeare or Beckett or John–*Paradise Lost*–Milton. (Does anyone know what the f*%k that book is about?)

357
You can't suddenly become a fan just because a team starts winning

Nobody likes a Jenny-from-Accounting-come-lately.

358
Don't say dumb stuff to derail a conversation about sports

Not every conversation has to be about you—accept that some people enjoy talking about sports and don't try to pull focus by feigning over-the-top ignorance: "Who's Stanley? What do you mean it's a cup? I thought a cup was the testicle protector thingy? Why would anyone want to win Stanley's cup? Sounds disgusting. See? This is why I don't follow sports."

Even if you genuinely don't know who or what the Stanley Cup is, you can probably figure it out by listening for context-based clues. So, don't be a dick, try harder.

359
Avoid jokes about soccer being a boring, low-scoring game where nothing happens

It's true, but it's a bit hack to make those kinds of jokes. I feel bad for including one here.

360
Don't pretend to like a team just because the guy you like likes them

Ladies, you know who you are, and this kind of behavior demeans us all.

SPECIAL RULES FOR MALE ATHLETES

361
Never assume a woman wants to have sex with you

Always ask the woman whether she wants to have sex with you. I know, it seems so obvious and yet . . .

362
Embrace the urge to get nude and sexual with your teammates

What I'm suggesting to you guys is, why not leave the woman out of it? I'm talking about those cases where multiple male athletes are alleged to have had group sex with one woman or when some of the team has hidden in a cupboard and watched while others have had sex with a woman. To me, it seems like sometimes the woman is only there to give the whole thing a thin veneer of heterosexuality and that you would probably all be quite happy just doing each other, and who can blame you? You're all elite-level athletes, you're all in great shape, you're all passionate about your game, and you love each other as pals. Why wouldn't you want to get physical with one another? In fact, it might even improve your performance as a team. It worked for the Spartans. Some historians believe it was actually all the man-love going on in that army that made them such a formidable fighting force.

After all, it's just sex, right—it doesn't mean anything (well, that certainly seems to be the attitude when there's a woman involved).

363
Never assume a woman wants to have sex with you

Oh hang on, I said this one already. You know what, I think it bears repeating. Always ask the woman whether she wants to have sex with you. And then maybe ask again just to make sure you heard her right.

PARTIES & CELEBRATIONS

A Word about Parties

I have never had a party. I've been to parties but I've never had a party, not even a twenty-first birthday. I had a "morning tea" instead. As a kid, my mother would give me the choice every year, "Do you want a birthday party, or would you rather go out for dinner with the family?" I chose dinner with the family every time. And yes, it was mostly because I loved dining at upmarket restaurants (like Pizza Hut), but I think there was also a nagging fear that I might have a party and no one would turn up. I've often wondered if that's where the whole routine of inviting the entire class stemmed from—perhaps it's nothing to do with not wanting to leave anyone out, and more about kids hedging their bets and making sure they get a decent turnout.

INVITATIONS AND ATTENDANCE

364
Late-notice cancellations can't be texted

If you want to cancel on the day of the event, you have to suck it up, make an actual phone call, and explain yourself. When you text through a last-minute cancellation, you revoke your right to be believed. Texted excuses are malarkey, everyone knows that.

365
Verbal invitations must contain specifics

It's quite common (and ill-mannered, according to my mother) to pose an invitation as a vague question. Something like:

"Hey! What are you doing Friday night?"

This puts the invitee in a real pickle. Do they admit to being free or not? What if you're about to invite them somewhere really great? They don't want to say "I'm busy" and risk missing out. On the other hand, what if it's an invitation to the Ruby Tuesday's where you'll get to watch Pam from Sales get wasted on dollar drinks while Brian from IT eats a steak bigger than his head.

The correct way to invite someone to something is to spell out all the details in your initial pitch, thereby leaving the invitee room to lie if they'd rather be dead than attend. For example:

"Hey! A bunch of us are going out for dinner on Friday night, Pam from Sales, Julia from Accounting, Sue from HR, the whole gang from IT, we're going to the Ruby Tuesday's. It's half-price cocktails between six and seven. Want to come?"

The person now knows everything they need to, and can confidently answer:

"Oh gosh, I'm sorry, I can't, I'm busy on Friday ... I have ... something going on. Bummer."

Always state your business up front and allow people plenty of room to invent an excuse if need be.

366
You don't have to farewell the entire room

Just say goodbye to the host and anyone else you happen to pass on your way out. You absolutely do not have to go around the entire party and farewell everyone you know. It should take you five minutes maximum to leave a party, not forty-five.

367
When cycling to events, take a few moments outside to recover before making your entrance

No one wants to kiss your sweaty cheek or shake your clammy hand.

BIRTHDAYS

368
A birthday text is sufficient

Let's be honest, no one really wants a birthday call. Let alone a string of them throughout the day. Except your mom. She's the exception—always call your mother on her birthday.

369
Facebook birthday greetings are insincere and meaningless

Everyone knows the reminder came up automatically on your Facebook feed and that you didn't actually remember yourself. By sending a Facebook message, you are simply acknowledging the fact that you forgot your friend's birthday. It's great to get that little reminder, but what you should do is remove Facebook from the equation and compose a birthday text message instead. That way you give the impression that it was you, not Mark Zuckerberg, who actually remembered this special day.

370
Don't mix your friends—have multiple birthday events instead

Intermingling of friends is hard work. And the onus to do all that work invariably falls on you as the single common denominator between people. So save yourself the trouble and schedule several birthday events instead.

DINNER PARTIES

371
If someone brings fancy wine to your dinner party, you must open it

Don't be one of those people (we all know them) who looks at the nice wine or Champagne they are handed on arrival and says, "Ooh, lovely!" and then puts it in a cupboard, clearly indicating they have no intention of opening it. White wine goes in the fridge; red wine stays on the kitchen counter—both these actions signal the "intent to serve." If it's a particularly special bottle and you don't happen to get around to serving it, the classy thing to do is keep it aside and bring it out the next time that person visits.

372
If you tell guests not to bring anything, don't be annoyed when they don't bring anything

373
If your host tells you not to bring anything, be sure to bring something

374
An intolerance is not an allergy

If you are allergic to shellfish or nuts or mutton chops, by all means inform your host because no one wants a dead dinner guest at the table, that's a real downer. Likewise, if you're going to swell up and turn purple, Violet Beauregarde-style, or break out in hives, then please make that information known ahead of time. But if you're calling your host to tell her that you're trying to "avoid carbs at the moment" then maybe it's better to just turn down invitations to dinner parties altogether.

375
Don't ostracize the vegan

I respect, nay, I applaud the lifestyle choice of the vegan. Vegans are only trying to make the planet a better place for everyone, so we must not mock and deride their decisions.

376
Vegans must lower their expectations

In return for my respecting a vegan's beliefs, I ask that the vegan respect my limited culinary abilities. For even though I am a decent cook, I do not have the skills or knowledge to make tasty vegan food. Vegetarian dishes I can whip up no problem, but if you take away my cheese and my yogurt and my honey and my eggs and basically every other ingredient in my fridge and pantry, then I'm afraid all I can offer you is a big bowl of air. My point is, I am happy to dine with vegans, I am happy to eat vegan food; however, you can't expect me to cook that food for you. The onus is on the vegan to source a restaurant with vegan options or invite me over for some tasteless chaff and beans. I promise I will smile politely and say, "Mmm, that's delicious, I think I can actually taste the planet being saved!"

377
Put some music on

Actually, this is not so much a rule as another one of my notes-to-self. I am notorious for hosting dinner parties and forgetting to create a bit of ambience. The thing is, I actually enjoy cooking in a nice quiet kitchen. Which is fine, provided I remember to put some music on when the guests arrive. No one wants to eat dinner accompanied only by the sounds of knives and forks scraping across plates and my recounting, in great detail, the latest series I watched on Netflix.

378
No hiving

"Hiving" is when you separate or "hive" someone off from the group and monopolize them. Couples who have been together a long time (like my parents) are notorious for this behavior. It occurs when one of the couple (usually my dad) is telling a story that the other one (usually my mom) has already heard and so to avoid having to sit through the story for the umpteenth time, the other one (my mom) "hives off" the person sitting next to her and starts up a separate and often intense one-on-one exchange. Hivers are the conversational equivalent of a defensive player in basketball who body-blocks their opponent and prevents them from getting involved in the normal run of play.

379
No more than six people at a dinner party

Sometimes you can't avoid big numbers, like at Christmas lunch or a family birthday, but when you are simply having a few people over for dinner, you should cap your guest list at six. Cooking for six is manageable. You'll have enough plates, you'll have enough serving dishes, and you shouldn't need to buy catering-size quantities of any ingredient.

More importantly, six is the magic number for dinner table conversation. Once you go over six guests, you end up with at least two conversations happening at the table and usually one of those conversations is far more interesting than the other. Invariably you will get stuck just out of range of *that* conversation and, what's worse, you could find yourself "hived off" by the really earnest guy who's married to your friend even though you've never known what she sees in him.

Meanwhile, you keep catching juicy snippets of the conversation happening at the other end of the table, involving someone who worked on a reality TV show or whose cousin went to school with Nicole Kidman and who, "swear to god," actually saw the ten-year marriage contract she had with Tom Cruise. At least that's what you think they're saying, it's hard to hear anything over the drone of the hiver.

380
Read the room, know when the party is over

Once the host has stopped opening wine and has moved on to serving hot beverages, chances are the party is winding down, so be on the lookout for further clues, such as the host yawning or leaving the table to start doing the dishes. If the conversation is cracking along and everyone's still having a great time, the only reason the host will leave the table is to open another bottle of wine.

And if the host goes to bed, party's over, get out.

WEDDINGS

381
One wedding is plenty

I don't care how many times you get married but you are only allowed one Billy Idol-style "white wedding," the type that comes with all that solemn gazing into one another's eyes vowing to take each other "in sickness and in health" and "till death do you part" business. When you've made such a grand to-do of promising to stay with someone until they're dead and then just a few years later, decide there's no way you can wait for this clown to die and you want a divorce, then you give up your right to make those sorts of melodramatic promises ever again. Because you clearly don't mean it. By all means, get married again and have a gathering to celebrate your union, but don't make everyone sit through another whole churchy wedding and earnest public declaration of your intent to see one another to the grave. And no more gifts. Enough with the gifts.

382
It's a wedding, not a GoFundMe campaign

If you say "Your presence is our present"—mean it. There should not be a hyperlink included on the invitation where guests can click and "donate now" to your honeymoon fund.

383
Don't be offended if you are not chosen to be bridesmaid

Rejoice.

384
Get an honest friend to review your
"self-penned" vows before the wedding

Writing your own vows is a difficult thing to do well. There's a reason those stock-standard vows became stock standards. The best self-written vow I've ever heard was from a woman who asked her partner to promise he would always swap meals with her if they were out at a restaurant and she was suffering from order-envy. He vowed that he would. I bet *they're* together till they die, because that is a really good vow.

385
No gift registries

Most couples these days have been living together for quite some time and already have a lot of stuff, so the wedding registry is really just two people wandering around a department store with a price scanner pointing and clicking at things they want but don't need. It's the equivalent of a child sitting on Santa's lap with an outrageous twenty-page list of demands for Christmas.

Getting married should not be viewed as an opportunity to refurbish your house with expensive items. If you can't afford to buy those things yourself, you shouldn't expect your friends to buy them for you either. If you *can* afford to buy them for yourself, then you should buy them for yourself.

To be clear, I'm not saying no gifts. I'm happy to buy you a gift, I just don't want to be handed a set of instructions on how to do it or how much you'd like me to spend.

I am well aware that hardly anyone else shares this view, which is why I have set up a special hotline. If you feel the need to vent your opinion about *my* opinion on gift registries, simply call *1(800) FUCK-YOU-FLANAGAN-I-LIKE-STUFF.*

386
Don't call it a wedding invite

It's an invitation. You invite people to your wedding with an invitation.

387
Be specific with your dress code

You can set any dress code you like for your wedding, just make sure you explain it fully. The more detail, the better. After all, most people, especially the ones reading this book, appreciate rules. And don't be afraid to use your wedding to enforce your personal moral codes on others, no matter how at odds they might be with current societal attitudes. Your day, your rules. For example, my wedding dress code would read: *You may wear a short skirt OR a low-cut top; you may not, however, wear both— let's keep it classy, ladies.*

388
One venue. No shuttle buses

Your friends will enjoy your wedding so much more if they don't have to move venues. Try to have the wedding and reception in the same place. I don't care how great the second venue is, if I have to get on a shuttle bus to get there then I'd rather stay put in the church parking lot and eat tacos from a food truck. After a few drinks, no one will care where they are anyway, so why not have everything all in one spot.

389
Treat your bridesmaids like grown-ups and don't put them in matching frocks

If you must follow "tradition" and have your bridesmaids in matching dresses, then do it properly. The custom hails back to Roman times when bridesmaids wore the exact same dress *as the bride*. It was done to create a bunch of decoys on the altar that would ward off evil spirits as well as confuse any angry, rejected suitors who might turn up wanting to harm the bride. So if you're not prepared to have all your gal pals in exactly the same fancy white dress as yours, then respect the fact that they all have different body shapes and different complexions and don't put everyone in the same strapless fuchsia bandage dress. You're not trying to recreate Robert Palmer's "Addicted to Love" video.

390
All you need is one good wedding photo

And that is a photo where you both look like decent versions of yourselves, where you both look happy to be there and neither of you have hair blowing across your face. Once you have that, relax, stand down the photographer, and head to the reception to be with your guests and enjoy your wedding.

The tediously long photo shoot with multiple locations is a construct invented by the wedding photographer to justify charging you an obscene amount of money. In this digital age when you can see the photos immediately and ascertain whether you have a good one, there is no longer any need to snap off hundreds of "just in case" photos. And there's certainly no need for a variety of backgrounds. Take the photos at the actual wedding venue and that way you'll remember the moment. You won't look back at photos in thirty years and say, "Hmm, I don't remember getting married on a cliff . . . or in a forest . . . or near a lake . . . or by the beach. Also . . . why are we jumping in the air? Was there a rat? Did the best man goose me?"

391
No one is fooled by the "candid" snap of a groom putting on cufflinks

All this photo says is "the photographer told me to look pensive and fiddle with my cufflinks."

392
The bride should remain vertical in all photos

Say no to any requests for a photo of the bride being held horizontal by all of the groomsmen. She's not a showgirl.

SPECIAL SEALED SECTION
WEDDING SPEECHES

I have sealed this section because I understand some people think there is no need for rules about wedding speeches. In fact, they believe the most entertaining part of a wedding is speech time, and by laying down a bunch of rules I am potentially ruining their opportunity to witness a classic train-wreck speech. And I understand your concerns but I don't think you need to worry. I once attended a wedding where the groom stood up and sang "Wind Beneath My Wings" acapella to his "beautiful lady" and no rule would ever have stopped him. He had a plan, he had a dream, and he was determined to see it through. Hats off to him. He sang from the heart, and it was one of the most memorable things I have ever seen. It was excruciating, but I wouldn't change it for the world. My point is, I'm quite happy for you to take or leave this next section, it's just here for anyone who would like a bit of help in avoiding being entertaining for the wrong reasons.

393
Five minutes, be funny, and get off

These were the inspiring words imparted to me by my mother as I stood up to make a speech at my sister's wedding. It was sound advice.

She also tapped her watch impatiently at me around the four-minute mark during my speech just in case I'd forgotten her instruction to "keep it tight."

It's a good idea to appoint a timekeeper for speeches— someone at the official table like a bridesmaid. She can ring a little bell when the speaker has one minute left. Because a good speech very quickly becomes a bad speech once it turns into a long speech.

394
Be relevant

It's not a twenty-first birthday party so forgo any hilarious stories about the bride or groom getting trashed and throwing up in a sink when they were fourteen. And it's not a lifetime achievement award either, no one is interested in a speech that chronicles every one of the bride's qualifications and accomplishments. Fathers tend to give this kind of LinkedIn profile speech when they think their daughter is too good for the man they are marrying. It's a passive-aggressive and public way of pointing out the disparity between the young lovers.

Finally, all anecdotes should be relevant in some way to the couple and/or their coupling, not just one of the individuals.

395
If you can't be funny, be sincere

I'm not suggesting you sing an acapella version of "Wind Beneath My Wings," but no one will judge you if you speak from the heart, especially if you keep it brief.

396
Sex plus time does not equal comedy

This advice is specifically for the best man.

It's best not to bring up any incident that involves the bride doing anything or anyone, no matter how long ago it might have been or how many years it was before she met the groom. It's still not funny—especially when her parents and grandparents are in the room. Likewise, ditch any references to the groom "banging" his way around Europe or to his lonely wanking days finally being over. Even if these tales killed at the bachelor party, they will never be funny at the wedding. Not for the right reasons anyway. If in doubt, leave out any story that features or even makes a vague reference to anyone's penis or vagina.

397
Lay off the booze until after you've given your speech

The more you drink, the funnier you think you are, and that's never a good thing when you're talking in front of an audience. It's always far better if the audience has had more to drink than you. So use your time wisely before the speeches: circulate and top up people's glasses.

398
Never start an anecdote with "Here's a funny story . . ."

This is a general rule for life, not only for wedding speeches. Better not to raise people's expectations unnecessarily. Just tell your story and let the audience decide for themselves whether it's funny or not.

399
Cap the number of speeches

No need to hear from everyone, it's not a congressional inquiry.

HALLOWEEN

400
No costume, no candy

This rule pertains to teenagers who suddenly think they are too cool to dress up but still want to go around panhandling for candy. You can't have it both ways, guys. The candy is the reward for dressing up. And that's why half-assed trick-or-treaters should be turned away empty-handed. And no, "plainclothes police officer" does not count as a costume. So either make an effort and wear a costume, or the only thing you're going home with is a bagful of air and disappointment.

401
Shut it down at 8 p.m.

Trick-or-treating needs a cut-off time. And I think 8 p.m. is the perfect time to call it a night. To encourage parents and children to stick to this curfew, I propose introducing a late-knock candy tax. Door-knock after 8 p.m. and the homeowner reserves the right to take a piece of candy from your bag instead of dropping one in.

402
Witches are scary, not sexy

No one minds when parents join in on the dressing up, provided they dress up as something befitting the scary Halloween theme. However, what is fast becoming the norm among the yummier of mummies is the sexy witch "costume"—which is really just mom in a short black dress, a pointy hat set at a jaunty angle, and a pair of too-high heels. Apart from there being no such thing as a sexy witch, Halloween is all about walking. You walk around the neighborhood knocking on doors asking for free candy. So wear appropriate footwear for such an event, and *remember you're out trawling for sugar for your kids, not a sugar daddy for yourself.*

403
Tell your kids to say "thank you"

In Australia, some people refuse to participate in Halloween, citing it as an American tradition that has no place here. I confess I used to be one of those people. The ones who turn out the lights, ignore the doorbell, and pretend not to be home. Silly really, not to mention, pointless. Because the Halloween genie is well and truly out of the bottle down under. Once Aussie kids found out about there was a holiday where you got to dress up and solicit the neighbors for free candy, there was no going back. What's not to like about costumes and free sugar? So a few years ago, I decided to stop being the neighborhood Grinch and embrace this newly imported tradition. Determined to join in, I decorated my house with foam skulls impaled on the iron railings of my fence (possibly a little too Atilla the Hun, but it was my first year, I was still learning) and bought a whole load of Furry Friends—which are flat thin bars of milk chocolate with unique Australian animals on the wrapper. I was joining in, yes, but I still wanted to make a cultural statement.

My first trick-or-treaters arrived at around 4:30 pm. I opened the door, admired their (fairly lame) costumes and offered them the bowl of Furry Friends. One child took a bar with a kookaburra on it, said nothing, and put it in her sugar sack; the other child took one, examined it, then looked up at me and said, "What is it?" I told her, "It's a Furry Friend, it's chocolate, with Wendy the wombat on the wrapper!" She wordlessly dropped it back into the bowl and returned empty-handed to her mother, who was waiting on the sidewalk. The child buried her head into mom's shoulder while mom patted her on the back and consoled her. Then they moved on the next house. Without a word?! At no point did anyone say "thank you." Not even the mother, she just shot me a withering look, as if to say, "I hope you're pleased with yourself because you and your stupid Furry Friends have just ruined Halloween!"

Point taken. Next time I'll be like my own mother who offers the kids orange segments as a "delicious treat." All the kids learned pretty quickly to give the "crazy fruit lady's house" a wide berth.

XMAS, NEW YEAR'S EVE, AND OTHER SPECIAL DAYS

404
Don't get a photo taken with Santa unless you're a child

The spontaneous "Hey! Let's get a photo with Santa" idea is only funny for you and your friend. No one else thinks it's cute or hilarious. Plus it's about thirty bucks. And you have to wait in line. Go have coffee and cake instead.

405
Firework displays should be three minutes maximum

After fireworks have been banging in the sky for a few minutes, you can really only see smoke anyway. And by the three-minute mark, we've pretty much seen all the color and shape combinations, it's now just variations on a theme and it stopped being in time with the simulcast soundtrack two minutes ago.

406
Enough with the exploding Harbour Bridge

This rule is for the Australian government: why don't you surprise the world one year by *not* firing a billion dollars' worth of fireworks off the Sydney Harbour Bridge?

407
You don't have to serve up a turkey

Some of us don't have a big enough oven to cook one. Some of us don't have a big enough family to eat one. And some of us just think turkey is totally overrated and wonder why we can't "give thanks" with fried chicken instead?

HOLIDAYS & TRAVEL

TRAVELING OVERSEAS

408
Never say you want to "do" a country

Say "I would like to go to Cuba" rather than "I really want to do Cuba." Doing a country sounds obnoxious and unnecessarily sexual.

409
Holiday attire is only for the holiday

For some reason, you can get away with a different look when you are away from home. But trust me, those batik fisherman's pants and man-beads you wore for ten days in Thailand or the acres of floaty linen and gold-roped espadrilles you wore around the resort in Los Cabos won't pass muster back home.

410
Dress appropriately for the country you are visiting

For example, a football jersey is not appropriate attire for visiting the Vatican. Tanks and flip-flops may be appropriate in Thailand or Bali, but if you are visiting a European capital city, probably best not to wear one of those gym singlets with the dropped armholes that show off your man nips. If in doubt, take your cue from the locals. Do the Parisian men have their man nips on display? No? Then put yours away.

411
Haggling is not compulsory

Before you dig your heels in and start trying to screw that local down in order to get yourself a bargain, do some math and convert the price to dollars. Then ask yourself, do you really need to save another six cents on a scrap of tie-dyed fabric that you plan to (but never will) turn into a cushion cover when you get home?

If you really must barter, then at least have the decency not to defend your quibbling by telling everyone, "Oh, but they expect you to haggle." I promise you no stallholder ever went home from a long day at the market with a bit of extra cash in his pocket bemoaning the fact that he was insulted by fleshy white people who paid full price and refused to honor the local culture by haggling.

412
You are not King Kong, you don't have to climb on or up everything

Sometimes it's nice to just look *at* things like the Eiffel Tower or the Sydney Harbour Bridge or Statue of Liberty or the Empire State Building rather than stand atop them. You are no less of a traveler because you didn't physically mount the landmark.

A Word about "Bunking In"

There is staying with friends (or relatives) and then there is "bunking in." It becomes bunking in the minute you have to get creative with sleeping arrangements, i.e. when there are more houseguests than there are bedrooms to accommodate them. Young people are excellent at bunking in because, for them, it's all about priorities. They will happily sleep in a bathtub if it means they have a few extra bucks to spend on something more important, like beer. I find country people are often very relaxed about bunking in too; they have a generous "the more the merrier" attitude toward it. I wish I could be like that, but unfortunately I'm a dyed-in-the-wool city mouse who'd rather sell her own grandmother to get cash for a hotel room than sleep on someone's floor and share one bathroom with ten people.

I have done my fair share of bunking in, most of it during a relationship I had with a guy whose entire extended family loved a bunk-in. It was actually their preferred style of accommodations, everyone all in together, sleeping wherever you land and not caring that unless you're up before dawn, you won't be getting a hot shower. Each holiday season, my partner and his kids, plus his two sisters, their partners, and their kids would set out on the annual pilgrimage to "Mom's place" on the coast. For two weeks, Mom's three-bedroom, one-bathroom bungalow housed seven adults, five children, and three youths. Youths, for those not familiar with the term, are male teenagers. Youths take up more space than children, and adults combined, not just with their lanky, overgrown limbs but with their excess energy. Youths can't sit still, they fidget, they knee-tremble, they bounce balls, they relentlessly click and unclick pens—and don't leave chopsticks within their reach or they'll be drumming on every available surface, including toddlers and slow-moving pets.

After participating in one of these holiday bunk-ins, I decided once was enough, and the following year I rented an Airbnb just down the road from Mom's. It had four bedrooms and two bathrooms and so long as I got the master bedroom with the en suite, I was happy to open the rest of the house up to all comers. Even the youths were welcome. I assumed I would be hailed a hero for providing all these extra rooms and beds, not to mention, showers and toilets.

Well, I couldn't have been more wrong. I immediately became the holiday pariah. My Airbnb was considered gratuitous and profligate. It was also deemed to be "miles from Mom's place" (for the record, it was fourteen houses away on the same street). And except for that master bedroom and en suite, the entire house went unused. No meals were cooked in the kitchen, no ablutions were performed in the bathroom, even the TV went unwatched. In fact, my own partner only stopped by, reluctantly, in the evenings to sleep and to shower. As soon as the sun rose, he was straight down to Mom's for bunk-in breakfast with the gang.

The year after that, right before the annual bunk-in, we broke up and he went to Mom's without me. I wasn't missed. To be honest, I'm not sure anyone even noticed I wasn't there—they probably all just assumed I was, once again, "miles away," holed up in my lavish and unnecessary Airbnb down the road.

HOUSEGUESTS

413
Three days only

This is not my rule by the way—this is accepted worldwide as standard. It's also ignored worldwide as standard.

I don't mind people coming to stay; I have a spare bedroom so no one has to bunk in, and I rather like having friends visit me. Three days is completely tolerable. However, after three days everyone starts to get on your nerves. For three days, you can put up with people not putting their breakfast comestibles away or leaving half-drunk cups of tea around your house or using all the hot water or putting dishes in the sink instead of the dishwasher. But any more than three days of that behavior and they start to feel like a shitty roommate rather than a guest.

414
Don't dominate the shared living spaces

This is particularly important if you are a young, male houseguest. As mentioned earlier, youths have an almost superhuman ability to spread themselves and take up all available space. A couch that would normally accommodate three adults comfortably looks positively crowded with only two youths on it.

415
Never come home empty-handed

Think of the money you are saving on accommodation and parlay that into a series of small gifts. After all, you'll only be there for three days, so that's not too much to ask. Basically, you should be proffering a token of appreciation each day, be it a bottle of wine or some nice fruit or a box of popsicles for the kids. This goes a long way to keeping your hosts happy and, more importantly, ensures they will have you back again rather than inventing some vague excuse as to why you can't stay next time. If you ever hear something like this, "Oh no, sorry, that week doesn't work for us because um ... yeah ... it just doesn't. Maybe next time," you know you've been a dud houseguest.

416
Leave on the day you said you would leave

A favorite trick of people who like free accommodation is to announce a change of circumstance mid-stay and then put the host on the spot by saying, "Oh, my flight was canceled" or "My other accommodation fell through," and then asking if they can stay an extra day or two. This fools no one. Your host knows what you're doing; they know that you know it's impossible to say no to your face, especially once you're already ensconced in the house. But while you might squeeze out a few extra nights on this visit, it's not really worth it because you risk being be barred from any future stays.

VISITORS TO AUSTRALIA

417
Don't plonk your towel uncomfortably close to someone else's

There should be only one question on the declaration form you complete before entering Australia:

"At the beach, how much space should you leave between your towel and that of a stranger?"

The answer is five feet. Minimum. And that is if the beach is crowded. If it's not, then anything less than ten feet is encroachment bordering on harrassment. There should be at least one whole towel length of clear space between your group and the next.

Australia has large beaches and plenty of them. There is always space, you might just need to walk a little further up the beach to find it. So don't be lazy, keep walking.

418
Vegemite is no big deal

It's just salty. And to any visiting celebrities, perhaps tell your publicist to ban "journalists" from asking you whether you've tried it yet. This is not for your sake—as I said, there's nothing wrong with Vegemite—it's more for the sake of the Australian viewing public. We are all sick to death of excitable journos asking celebs, "Have you tried Vegemite? Oh my god! What did you think of it?!" No one cares. And for the record, a lot of Australians don't like it either. (I'm not one of them by the way, I love the stuff.)

THE ARTS

A Word about "Culture"

Most of us happily ignore galleries and museums until we are overseas, when we are suddenly struck by an overwhelming and oppressive obligation to do things we would never normally do, like visit museums and art galleries.

Friends of mine are appalled when I admit that I don't really want to line up to go to MoMA or the Guggenheim or even the Louvre. I'm not against art or old stuff, I'm simply not into waiting in lines. If I could just wander in and do a quick lap when I happened to be in the area, I'd do it for sure, but that's not an option. Places are so busy now, you have to plan your visit in advance, which usually includes pre-purchasing your ticket. However, even with a pre-purchased ticket you still have to line up to get inside, and then, once inside, you are herded through the halls and exhibits by staff barking at you to "Keep moving folks, keep moving!" It's just not a fun day out when you factor in all the waiting and the yelling, especially when the only reward is a room full of old bowls and spoons and bits of flint.

These days I tend to travel mostly with my sister, because she holds no truck with galleries and museums either. She is unapologetic about the fact that she would rather go for lunch at a diner or spend an afternoon shopping at Bloomingdale's than shuffle around a museum pretending to be fascinated by armless statues and ancient ewers. She would rather have a cocktail in a bar with a view of the Empire State Building than stand in line to go up the Empire State Building and then look down at the many places below where one could be enjoying a cocktail.

But if you can't avoid it and you find yourself being dragged around an art gallery or museum, you will no doubt benefit from the following rules.

MUSEUMS AND ART GALLERIES

419
It is worth waiting in line for a natural history museum

I realize I just said I don't like waiting in line, but I make an exception for natural history museums because I really like dinosaur skeletons and I'm fascinated by things preserved in jars of formaldehyde. Also you get to see a whole bunch of creepy taxidermied creatures that, for some reason, are always posed so as to appear threatening. Even the sweetest-looking little desert mouse becomes menacing when he's stuffed and stood on his hind legs with his little pointy teeth bared. I wish that was an option for people. I don't really fancy being buried or cremated, but I'd love to be stuffed and placed in an exhibit at the natural history museum; I could be posed sitting cross-legged, mouth slightly open, staring glassy-eyed at a television, a true representation of the twenty-first-century human.

420
Stand back from the exhibit

It's an artwork, not the baggage carousel. Don't bunch around it and prevent others from getting a decent look.

421
Don't take photos of a painting

Taking a photo of a famous painting on your phone is almost as stupid as going to a live concert and filming it instead of watching it. When has anyone ever sat down to watch the brilliant concert footage they filmed on their iPhone from Row W? If a painting is so famous that you want a picture of it, there's every chance you'll be able to find a much better image online or

275

in postcard form at the gift shop on the way out. Trust me, no one wants to look at your bad photo of a painting. A painting which is probably behind glass anyway so all you've really managed to capture are the reflections of other people gathered around taking photos of the painting.

Seriously, there's no need to take pictures of pictures. It's really dumb.

422
Go with someone who has the same boredom threshold as you

The minute I set foot in a gallery or museum, I check my watch and start thinking about how long I have to wait before I can suggest we find the cafe and have coffee and cake. I usually last about fifteen minutes, which means I need to be with a friend who has the same low tolerance level as me, because when I turn around and say, "Should we get cake?" I want an enthusiastic thumbs up, not a withering look that tells me I'm an uncultured swine with no appreciation of fine art.

423
Think twice before purchasing in the gift shop

I understand everyone likes a souvenir, at the very least you want something that reminds you of the time you waited in line for two hours in order to get into the Louvre where you quite possibly motored your way directly to the *Mona Lisa* and came straight back out again. (No judgment from me.)

Once you are in the gift shop, however, it's easy to get a bit giddy and overexcited—for a start, it means you're almost out of there—but don't get carried away. Stop and consider the artist for a moment when you're browsing through the endless merchandise available. Ask yourself, is it what da Vinci would have wanted? His artwork printed on a tote bag that will be used to cart around your stinky yoga clothes? His artwork on a beach towel that will be used to rub down a half-naked, salty, sandy person? Maybe just buy a postcard—it's bound to be better than that photograph you took on your phone.

424
Not all of your thoughts need to be articulated

This is a rule for a certain type of tourist (often American but not always) who doesn't seem to understand that it's okay for some of your thoughts to remain thoughts. There's no need to provide a running commentary on everything you're seeing and doing. Perhaps just try seeing and doing. For example, when I went to see the Book of Kells exhibition at Trinity College Library in Dublin, everyone managed to enjoy the display in respectful silence. Except for Harry and Lorraine from Iowa who felt the need to play a loud game of "say what you see" as they waddled around the hall. Here are a few fun facts Lorraine felt she should share with everyone else in the room, just in case we were all illiterate and couldn't read the same information panel she was now reading.

"Monks wrote this book? Monks? Can you believe it, Harry? It was monks!?"

Lorraine was so impressed by the fact that monks wrote the book that I started to wonder whether she thought "monks" was actually an Irish word for monkeys. She was then struck by something else incredibly fascinating.

"They wrote it by heee-yand [hand], Harry, this whole book, all by heee-yand, can you believe it?" For some reason she seemed surprised that these ninth-century monks (or monkeys?) weren't using Microsoft Word.

Basically, the rule is, not every thought has to be vocalized and it certainly doesn't have to be vocalized at volume.

THE ZOO

I realize that zoos are a contentious issue—none of us likes to think about wild animals being kept in cages. That said, I just love animals so much that if there's a chance to see some, even if they're in cages, I'll take it. When I am on tour, if I have time, I like to seek out the local zoo and go look at animals. Any animals. I even like the boring, smelly mountain goats, the way they stand awkwardly on top of rocky outcrops and seem to have no other purpose in life but to cover the ground with their pellety poo. As for meerkats, I can watch those things for hours. But my favorite exhibit of all time has to be the African painted dogs at the Perth Zoo. Nice one, Perth Zoo, double thumbs up.

And while I have always enjoyed the city of Wagga Wagga (they have some excellent restaurants and cafes and a terrific arts center), I must say they are drawing a very long bow in claiming to have a zoo. But claim they do. It's listed prominently on the visitor information leaflet, and there are quite a few signs up around the town directing you to the Wagga Wagga Zoo. The problem is, there's no zoo. There's a peacock, a pig, and a couple of ducks. So my first rule is:

425
Birds plus a farm animal do not maketh a zoo

It's not just Wagga—a lot of small towns claim to have a zoo when all they have is a sheep, a goat (regular, not mountain), and a few geese. Technically, that's a small farm. To be classified as a zoo, you must have something larger than a cow, like an elephant. Or something that can eat you, like a bear or a lion.

And no, I'm afraid exotic birds don't count—that's an aviary, not a zoo. If it's a place that only has native animals, that's okay but maybe call it a "wildlife sanctuary," so I can lower my expectations before I get there. For example, "Tamworth Marsupial Park" leaves prospective guests in no doubt as to what they should expect. And it really makes a difference. I went in expecting marsupials, I got those critters in spades, and I enjoyed my visit immensely. Five stars.

426
No talking

Before I get called a Grinch, this is a rule for adults, not children. Children sound a lot like chattering monkeys when they are excited, and that's completely appropriate at the zoo, therefore I have no problem with it. It's the endless and senseless educational monologuing from parents at the zoo that I find tedious. At every single exhibit you are forced to listen to adults jabbering away, trying to turn a fun day out at the zoo into a series of teachable moments. "Do you know what this animal is, Jacob? It's a lion. What noise does a lion make? Can you roar like a lion, Jacob? Can you see the lion? Do you think he might be hiding?"

I guarantee you the lion is hiding, Jacob, inside his cave with his paws over his ears, rocking back and forth, going, "Make it stop, Jacob, please make the grown-up stop talking!"

The zoo is already fun, there is already plenty to do and see, so relax, mom and dad, dial down the audible parenting. You've done your job by bringing the child to a stimulating environment, you don't need to constantly badger them with questions and knowledge and learning.

427
No tapping

This is a rule for both adults and children. Zoos have a way of bringing out the dumbest behavior in humans. It's as if this visual reminder that we are at the top of the food chain makes us so arrogant that we forget how to behave in a civilized fashion—from tapping on the glass to "wake" up the animals to climbing into enclosures in order to get a selfie with a bear. If you get eaten at the zoo because you climbed over a fence, that's called natural selection and the world won't miss you.

THE THEATER

428
Leave at intermission if you're not enjoying it

If the play is rubbish in the first half, it's unlikely it will suddenly pick up in the second half, so it's perfectly acceptable to cut your losses and leave at intermission. You're actually doing the producers a service as it's the only discreet way to send a message that the play is not up to scratch and needs work.

The problem is theater audiences are incredibly polite and invariably they will still clap at the end of a play whether it's good or bad. And because all clapping sounds the same, the actors have no way of telling whether the applause indicates enjoyment or simply relief that the play is over.

Comedians are possibly the only performers who constantly get honest feedback. When audiences don't enjoy comedy, they don't laugh, which is a clear indicator to the comedian that they are not being funny. Sometimes an audience member will go even further and actually yell out exactly what they think of the comedian. And while it can be alarming to be told that "You're shit!" it's also the quickest way to learn not to be shit. Playwrights and actors don't enjoy the benefit of that kind of honest feedback so a walkout at intermission is the kindest thing you can do for them.

BOOKS

429
Never tell someone the book (or movie) has a twist

This ruins the whole book, because the person then spends their whole time reading, thinking, *Ooh, I wonder if this is the twist?*

430
Don't say you hate Kindles because you "love the smell of books"

If you're such a big reader, you should have a lower tolerance for clichés.

431
If you borrow a book, return it promptly

Conversely, if you lend someone a book, be prepared never to see it again.

432
Don't recommend award-winning literature to make yourself appear smart

If you genuinely enjoyed it, by all means pass on your recommendation, but don't just pretend you liked it because you think you will sound dumb if you admit you didn't really get it and that you found the language incredibly dense to the point of being impenetrable.

433
Celebrity is not a synonym for children's book author

I imagine being a celebrity is an eventful and satisfying job. There are parties and openings to attend, products to hock, and heavily filtered Instagram photos to post. So why not leave the children's book market to the children's book authors. Just a thought.

SPECIAL REMOVABLE SECTION
REALITY TELEVISION

Reality TV is more popular now than ever before, which is astonishing. I naively assumed that once people had seen reality TV and realized how it works, these shows would disappear from our screens. Because surely after you've seen a show like The Bachelor *or* My Kitchen Rules *or* Married at First Sight *and watched how people are portrayed as either idiots or assholes (or sometimes both) you couldn't possibly be convinced to sign up for one. I figured that by season three of any reality show, they'd be forced to cast Amish folk because they'd be the only people in the world oblivious to the machinations of shows like Twenty Desperate Women in Polyester Dresses Competing for One Incredibly Dull Man in a Tuxedo.*

Turns out, I'm like Jon Snow: I know nothing. And in fact, applications for these shows are on the rise. Where once the standard response to, "Would you like to go on television, be made to look stupid, have the worst side of yourself on display, and be publicly humiliated?" would have been "No thanks, I'd rather be dead," these days, more and more people are up for it. Apparently, the lure of Insta fame, at whatever price, is too attractive.

So if you happen to know one of these bizarre individuals who aspires to be on reality TV, feel free to remove this section

*from the book and give it to them. It might help them to avoid
looking like a total dick. The key word there is "might." There
are no guarantees. Very few people come out of these shows
looking good, which brings us nicely to the most important rule
of reality television:*

434
The producer is not your friend

Never forget that, not even for a minute. Off-screen, they'll pretend
to care, they'll pretend to be your buddy, but on-screen you are
going to be stitched up and presented as either contemptible or
crazy. The producers will always find a way to make you look stupid,
whether it's through guile, fatigue, or just plying you with alcohol.

Even if you do manage to keep it together during filming, even
if you stay alert and keep yourself nice, even if you don't give
producers what they want on tape, they will find a way to get
you in the edit. You can't win. The only sure-fire way to beat the
producer and come out looking like a decent person, is to say,
"No, I do not wish to participate in this program."

435
Have a killer backstory

Whatever show you're going on, make sure you have a backstory
that involves either something sad, like an ailing grandmother,
or something titillating, like escaping from a cult. It will not only
guarantee you get cast but it will also make it harder for people
to hate you on social media. People will still find a way to hate you
on social media, but at least you'll make it more difficult for them.

LOVE SHOWS

436
Never say "I have a lot of love to give"

Sounding off about having a lot of love to give makes it sound like you have a virulent STD just waiting to be transferred. Or that you have a massive surplus of love because no one has ever wanted to take it from you.

437
Avoid the clichés

The most tiresome cliché trotted out on these shows is the one where someone says they are "afraid to open up because they've been hurt before." This is complete poppycock. The real reason that person is not opening up is because they are not in any way attracted to the love object on offer.

The right thing to do in this instance is stop boring us with your trite soundbites, admit the other person doesn't blow your skirt up, and exit the show. Unless, of course, you didn't *actually* go on the show to find love? But who would do that?

438
Don't mention your walls

There are more references to walls on *The Bachelor* and *Married at First Sight* than there are on *The Block*. Everyone has their walls up these days. Maybe that's why they've all got "so much love to give"— it's been piling up behind those walls unable to escape. But I'm afraid you can't talk about having your walls up while simultaneously allowing dozens of cameras to film everything you do and say.

439
No need to mention how important your kids are to you

Especially when you've just abandoned them for an indefinite period of time in order to follow your dream of becoming a celebrity by appearing on a reality TV show—a show where your kids will get to watch you behave like an undignified tit, say embarrassing things, and quite possibly open-mouth kiss a stranger on national television. If you really love your kids, don't search for a new partner on a reality TV show.

RENOVATION SHOWS

440
Stop installing black faucets

Honestly, that stuff is going to look dated before this book has even hit the shelves. Same goes for rose gold faucets.

441
No stupid giant overhead shower heads

Women hate them. They might look much more fancy than a standard shower head on an adjustable arm, but they're really annoying because the water just rains down all over your head, which means you have to wear a shower cap every time.

442
You can't improve on the light switch

Imagine this scenario: you walk into a room, it's dark, you flick a switch on the wall, the room lights up. Magic. The light switch is one of the greatest inventions of all time, the very definition of practicality and functionality. And yet contestants on renovation shows are always desperate to replace light switches with complicated technology like C-Bus or those creepy Alexa Google robot things? I can't see what advantage is gained by entering a room and shouting (slowly and deliberately) into the air, "Alexa—turn—on—my—living—room—light!" It's no faster than flicking a switch. It's lazy, in that you literally can't be bothered lifting a finger, not to mention it's also advocating bad manners, because no one ever says "please" or "thank you" when they order Alexa the Google Robot to turn on the lights. Ultimately it seems to indicate people's impolitic desire to return to the days of having servants and slaves to do your bidding for you.

443
No one needs a "reading landing"

A reading landing is both pointless and pretentious. It's actually just a flat part at the top of the stairs furnished with a comfy chair that no one will ever sit on and a bookshelf filled with books that no one will ever read.

COOKING SHOWS

First of all, let me say I am impressed by anyone who can cook under pressure and within a certain timeframe. While I am fairly confident that I could attempt any recipe, I would need all day to do it. And there's no way I could cook with a clock counting down and judges yelling at me that my time was nearly up. I'd have a meltdown and end up in the fetal position on the bench with my head in a George Foreman grill. So I admire anyone who can cook under time pressure (which, I guess when you think about it, is pretty much any decent chef in a decent restaurant).

444
Cook with ingredients and utensils

Every season we see a slew of contestants who claim to "cook with love" and then wonder why they don't win the show. I've made plenty of cakes in my time, some good, some okay, some disastrous. And with regard to those baking disasters, the problem always came down to my not paying enough attention to the recipe or not being precise enough with my measurements. Throwing in an extra cup of love would not have made a bit of difference.

It's the same when friends come over for dinner. Sometimes they ask for the salt or the pepper, but no one has ever said, "Kitty, this mutton stew is really unpleasant, I think it needs more love? Do you have any love in your pantry? Don't get up, just tell me where it is, I'll get it."

445
If in doubt, roll Nonna out

Even if you didn't have a nonna that sat you on her lap and taught you how to roll pasta or make cannoli, invent one, especially if you think you're about to flame out in a challenge. Take your food up to the tasting bench and tell them it's your grandmother's secret recipe and that it's a traditional dish passed down over generations. The judges never trash old ladies' recipes, especially when they're from another country; it would make them seem culturally ignorant or insensitive.

446
Stop saying your dream is to open a dessert bar

Dessert bars are only a good idea on paper or *maybe* in New York where there are millions of people and the city never sleeps (™Frank Sinatra). But anywhere else, forget it. For a start, no one wants to move venues to have dessert. Changing venues kills the vibe. Also, the minute you try to move a group en masse, you lose people. Once everyone is out on the street debating the best way to get to this dessert bar—"Can we walk? How far is it? Do we need two cabs?"—it all becomes too hard and people just go home.

And for people like me who often finish work late and have trouble finding a restaurant that is still open and serving food (because I live in Sydney, an international city, where restaurant kitchens close at 9 p.m.), the dessert bar is a cruel illusion. The doors are open, the lights are on, it looks like food is still being served, so you start to think you might actually be able to get a meal, only to walk in and be crushed by the news that "Yes, we are still serving but . . . we only do desserts."

THE FINAL RULE

447
Lower your expectations, that way you can never be disappointed

Some of you may have been expecting a few more rules—after all, it says 488 on the cover. Honestly though, I'm amazed and also slightly alarmed that I made it this far. I knew I had a lot of rules but I had no idea I had this many.

If you're wondering why the title isn't *447 Rules for Life*, it's because—as I mentioned in the introduction—this book was only ever supposed to be a joke. For the purposes of a comedy segment, I picked a large random number that I thought sounded funny. Once it turned into a real book, however, I found I'd become strangely attached to that arbitrary number, 488, and didn't want to change it.

And since embarking on this project and discussing it with everyone I meet, I've discovered that everybody has a rule about something. I guarantee that the minute you finish this book you will, no doubt, start thinking of other rules I should have included.

Hang on, there was no rule about how often you should change the sheets?

or

Why didn't she include a rule about not putting parmesan cheese on seafood pasta?

or

Seriously? No rule about always wiping front to back. She's dead to me.

So these last few pages are for you, the owner of this compendium, to fill in whatever rules you think I have omitted. They can be completely logical or totally insane. You'll get no judgment from me; in fact, I promise to endorse any and all additions, no matter how nutty. Add as many as you like, because one rule I admit I did forget to include is that you can never have too many rules.

INSERT YOUR OWN RULES FOR LIFE

- -

- -

- -

- -

- -

- -

- -

- -

- -

- -

- -

- -

Acknowledgments

The first person who gets a thank-you is obviously Mr. Jordan Peterson. It's no secret his book inspired mine—I'm just glad he stopped at twelve and left the rest for me.

I need to thank the fabulous ladies at Allen & Unwin: Kelly Fagan for pushing me to write this book and Angela Handley for pushing me to stop writing this book and finish it already; thank you, Angela, you've been incredibly patient.

Thanks to my fellow rule-makers, Sophie, Penny, and Rozie, not only for your excellent contributions but also for helping to keep this book from becoming the insane rantings of a middle-aged lady. (I hope.)

Bruce Griffiths always deserves my thanks, for suggestions, contributions, and for being someone who loves rules as much as I do.

To my best friend Glenn, thank you for sharing the knowledge on what it takes to be a good conversationalist and for generously participating in the many tour-van chats I hijacked and made all about me and my rules book.

Thanks to Nina Oyama, for being my totally shmood youth-speak consultant. (I know, I know, I'm not using shmood correctly.)

Tom Peterson, my producer on The Weekly, *thank you for the brilliant job you did on the 488 Rules segment, you made people want a book that didn't exist. Well played.*

To Tohby Riddle, who designed the book and did the illustrations. You're such a class act and the best kind of perfectionist. I heart you.

Thank you to my dad, who assured me that no one ever turns their book in on time and said I wasn't to let anyone rush me. (This from a man who has never missed a deadline.)

Nothing I do would be possible without the support of A-List Management—Artie Laing, you are a diamond, and Karen Laing, please promise you will never leave me.

Finally, to Joel, my unicorn, thank you for always being so incredibly supportive. I don't know how you tolerate so many rules yet somehow you do—well, except for number 191. But I know you're working on that one, and I appreciate it. xx

ABOUT THE AUTHOR

Kitty Flanagan is one of Australia's best-known comedians. She appears on TV regularly but spends most of her time touring the country doing stand-up.

She has two dogs, one cat, and a dishwasher that she loves more than all of her pets combined. Her favorite food is soup. 488 Rules for Life *is her second book.*

Also by Kitty Flanagan

Bridge Burning and Other Hobbies—
a collection of funny true stories